# Team Secrets
## of the Navy SEALs

# Team Secrets
## of the Navy SEALs:

*The Elite Military Force's Leadership Principles for Business*

### Anonymous

**Andrews McMeel
Publishing**

Kansas City

03 04 05 06 07 EBI 10 9 8 7 6 5 4 3 2 1

Library of Congress Cataloging-in-Publication Data

Anonymous.
    Team secrets of the Navy SEALs : the elite military force's leadershi
principles for business / Anonymous.
        p. cm.
    ISBN 0-7407-1907-6
    1.Teams in the workplace. 2. Leadership. 3. United States. Navy. SEALs.
I.Title: Elite military force's leadership principles for business. II.Title.

HD66.N44 2003
658.4'02–dc21

                                                          2002044061

Book design and composition by Just Your *Type*.

# CONTENTS

# ABOUT THE AUTHOR

The author of *Team Secrets of the Navy SEALs*
is a seasoned professional in the U.S. military's elite
fighting force. All names will be kept secret to protect him,
his fellow members of the Naval Special Warfare community,
their families, their superiors, and their missions.

# INTRODUCTION:
## Background of the Teams

Since the establishment of our force, Frogmen have willingly put themselves at risk so that others may live free and fruitful lives. The men of Naval Special Warfare are willing to go where and do what others cannot or will not.

Naval Special Warfare has always been and always will be a strictly volunteer organization. If at any time a Frogman wishes to leave, he may do so. When a Team member is unwilling to complete an assigned task, there is no sense in bringing him along; others are already waiting for the opportunity to prove their mettle. This important parallel to the business world is the basis of the lessons in this book.

In World War II, U.S. forces took heavy losses because of their inexperience with amphibious operations and at acquiring intelligence. Procuring information about the composition of beachheads, the firmness of the sand, and the location of sandbars, coral reefs, and man-made obstacles became absolutely imperative. The technology behind today's satellites, which provide immediate and up-to-date imagery, was still decades away. The question was how to get such detailed and current information. The answer was Naval Combat Demolition Units (NCDUs), amphibious reconnaissance forces that operated in advance of conventional troops, at great personal risk.

These Frogmen were men so dedicated to their country that they were willing to do whatever was asked of them. They often went into combat wearing only swim trunks, a knife, a mask, fins, and a satchel of explosives. This earned them several names, the two most noted and cherished being "naked warriors" and "Frogmen." In a time before wet suits, these men of iron resolve would cover their bodies with axle grease to fight off the bone-chilling waters of the Atlantic.

Over time, the forces became known as UDTs (Underwater Demolition Teams). During the Korean War the UDTs began a transition to hinterland operations, conducting small demolition raids. After the Korean War the need for antiguerrilla warriors was recognized. In 1961 President Kennedy commissioned the first two SEAL Teams (Sea, Air, Land Teams) to conduct "unconventional warfare." (SEAL Team One was based on the West Coast, SEAL Team Two on the East Coast.) UDTs were still in existence; however, they were slowly phased out over the next few decades as more SEAL Teams were commissioned.

SEALs saw their first combat during the Vietnam War, earning them a reputation as the most ruthless operators, accepting and completing missions that others would not even consider. Although SEALs were killed, not one was ever left behind or captured. This is a fact that all SEALs value and live by, and it is the basis of the Team concept.

From the very first days of the Frogman lineage up to the time this book was published, only 240 classes and a handful more than 6,500 men have made the grade.

To date, not one man involved in a SEAL operation has ever been left behind.

# CHAPTER 1
## Leading the Best

## Navy SEALs Concepts for Leading Professionals and Team Building

Every moment of a SEAL's life is geared toward the Team! The word *Team* encompasses everything from the platoon to our entire country. In the Teams, men work relentlessly with their Teammates and face incredible odds to accomplish their missions.

What would you think if your boss told you that you were going to push a boat out of an airplane at night and then jump out after it, deploying your own parachute and chasing the boat to the water with seven other people and without the help of any lights? Next, you'll need to maneuver out of your parachute and get the boat operational in ten minutes, because you have to pick up eight more men who are about to jump into the water. Then you'll have to paddle for several hours and rendezvous at a predesignated meeting point—all under the cloak of one night's darkness. A sixteen-man Team—two officers and fourteen enlisted men—complete all the planning, preparation, coordination, supervision, and execution of such a mission.

That mission is just the one you'll be doing this week. Every day of this week and the next, and the next after that, you will be responsible

1

for the lives of your Team members, either in training or in combat. The only way you can survive is to trust your Team and be trusted by them. You can't think only of yourself. Everyone's life depends on each member thinking as a Team. This is my life, and this is how I survive. The principles of SEAL Team leadership and cohesiveness apply to all Teams; and strong Teams, in business and in life, are ruthlessly effective in achieving their common goals.

I am an active-duty Navy SEAL and will not use my real name or that of any of my brothers. Many of my closest friends are also still on active duty, and it would be inappropriate to proffer their identities as well. I have built this book, however, with stories from my own experience. Lead by example, build a stronger Team, and over time you will create a successful business and career.

## Basic Philosophy of the Teams: Volunteer Program

To get a shot at SEAL training, you must exhibit initiative and determination. It isn't easy to get into BUD/S (Basic Underwater Demolition/SEAL), which is the initial training prospective SEALs must go through. Determination is the key. Out of about every three hundred men who say they want to be SEALs, probably one hundred mean it and only about twenty actually make the necessary effort. The day I tested, only five of seventeen sailors passed the initial screening for BUD/S. And even then inclusion was not guaranteed. It took me over eight months to convince my command to let me go and secure orders to BUD/S.

Over a year after my initial screening I arrived in sunny Coronado, California, to attend BUD/S at the Naval Special Warfare Center. My class started with 129 men who swore they wouldn't quit. After seven months, 114 couldn't keep their word.

The daily BUD/S schedule was part of the reason. In First Phase, the initial aspects of Team building weed out those who do not belong. The days and nights are filled with a series of physical challenges, called evolutions, performed in a continuous rotation. During the right of passage called Hell Week, a man might get an hour and a half of sleep from Sunday morning to Friday evening, all the while working nonstop.

In Second Phase, the physical standards get tougher and an intense diving curriculum begins. The underwater aspect of SEAL operations is extremely serious, and those who don't have the physical stamina or can't keep their wits about them underwater in the pitch dark tend to volunteer to leave the program here.

Third Phase demands that sailors reach the highest physical and mental standards. Not many men are lost during this time, however, because those who would prefer another profession and those who could not meet the strength requirements have already quit.

Throughout this training, SEAL instructors never let you forget that you are seeking membership in a volunteer organization. They realize that they may someday work with you and that their lives will depend on your competence. They have a vested interest in the quality of their students. In the meantime, they continually monitor those who are wavering and offer to help these men find a niche in the Navy if it turns out that being a SEAL is not their priority.

## Team Concepts for the Individual: *Never Quit!*

If you have been assigned a task, you had better seriously evaluate your ability to complete it. There is no honor in accepting a remarkably daunting task if you can't get it done *correctly*. Lives depend on you. You should not shelter yourself in menial tasks but should carefully assess all situations and take on any challenge you feel able to accomplish. Moreover, remember that once you have committed, you are in. If you suddenly find that you're in over your head, you had better sprout gills and come up with a way to finish the job.

The point to the intensity of any training program is, and should be, to identify those who are going to work when it counts. Job titles may sound glamorous, but you need to know who is going to be there when the Team needs them the most.

## You Are Only as Strong as Your Weakest Team Member

"Weakest" may simply refer to the Team member carrying the heaviest load. In a SEAL platoon, the communications man usually carries the most weight, because of his radios and extra batteries. He is not weak, but he will most likely be the slowest and most encumbered member. If the point man (usually the person with the lightest load) leading the Team maintains a rapid pace, he will likely exhaust and unnecessarily wear out this important "Comm Guy."

A Team leader will have a reason for picking each member of the Team. Recognize the attributes on which you based your choices. Make sure that all Team members know that others depend on them and that they are expected to act accordingly. You must surround yourself with "operators"—those who perform—always being mindful of the difference between the man you'd like to have around and the one you and your Team need. Job assignment is not a popularity contest; you should always choose the best person for each job.

One important thing to remember: Just because someone is new doesn't mean he will not be able to improve upon the way business is conducted. I have noticed that at times "old guys" will ignore the "new guys" simply because they are new. *Never* underestimate the value of a fresh, innovative, and perhaps even abstract point of view. Diversity is good and can strengthen the Team.

## SEAL Training and Common Goals

SEAL instructors stress the Team concept from the beginning. Everything is done as a class. Men eat as a class, train as a class, work out as a class, learn as a class, and "pay the man" as a class. If one man screws up (the weak link for that evolution), everyone joins him in performing the assigned penalty, thereby motivating the entire Team to mend the weak member's ways. You fall as a Team and succeed as a Team.

A BUD/S class is broken down into Boat Crews of six or seven men, fewer when several people quit. As the name suggests, each Team has the charge of a boat. An IBS (inflatable boat, small) resembles a white-water raft. Two of the most memorable Team-building exercises are Log P.T. (physical training) and surf passage. Log P.T. is done as a Boat Crew with a fifteen-foot section of a telephone pole. The instructors run the men through a series of exercises with the log, each requiring the efforts of the entire Boat Crew. If one person slacks off from his job, the others will feel how they are required to labor under the added weight.

For example, in such exercises as sit-ups, each man cradles his section of log in his arms, holding the log over his head until the instructor gets tired of watching them. My personal "favorite" was the foot races in soft sand with the log on the men's shoulders. In order for the entire crew to "get on the log," they'd have to turn their bodies forty-five degrees to one side, which made it even harder to run. The crew was jammed on the log and it took maximum Team coordination to prevent feet from entangling and bringing the crew to the ground in a pile of limbs followed closely by the three-hundred-pound log. Oftentimes the entire Boat Crew had to hold the log overhead, arms extended, for one minute. Arms and shoulders would be depleted of strength and many crews would fail this test repeatedly. Crews could not leave until they completed this task. I can remember occasions when it took my crew a dozen attempts before success—we would wonder how we got it the twelfth time but couldn't do it the first time. That is what BUD/S and Team building is all about—persevering until success!

In surf passage, the Boat Crew is required to paddle its boat through the pounding surf zone to the relative calm of the waters beyond. One man calls the cadence while the rest paddle in unison to attain this common goal. This is a difficult evolution during the winter months because the waves are huge and can easily mangle the boats. If one man stops paddling while tackling a wave, the entire crew will pay as the powerful wave tosses them about like rag dolls.

## It Pays to Be a Winner!

Certain evolutions in BUD/S pit the Boat Crews against one another in healthy competition, commonly in the form of races, where the men run while carrying either the boat or the log as a crew or paddle to designated points. The winning Boat Crew is usually rewarded by an early release from the exercise or the chance to sit out the next race.

In Naval Special Warfare, officers and enlisted men endure the exact same training. Team members can't help but form ties when they work closely together. All members of the Team have the same training, and though some men hold positions of leadership, they are, first and foremost, members of the Team.

## Natural Selection

Through these activities, the Teams inevitably shed some weight. As members of the Boat Crews drop out, new Teams form. It is imperative that the new crew members adapt and learn one another's strengths and weaknesses, and prepare to face the instructor's next labyrinth of trials. It's all business—the individual does not have the luxury of mourning his buddy who decided to quit. At every turn, each man is reminded that he is there because he wants to be. A man can stop the pain and stress whenever he wants to, simply by telling the instructors that he has had enough and wishes to quit.

## Results

As a professional, you have a job to do. The previous examples of Team building may seem like excessively harsh training that results in staggering attrition, but such culling is necessary if you want to select only those who will not quit when it counts. The purpose of weeding out the unfit is strikingly evident when you proudly sit among those who've decided to stay and work for the Team.

If you make it through all the trials, you join a Team made up of life-long friends, with a "sea bag" full of confidence, an enhanced appreciation for the human spirit, and an unrivaled sense of what a true Team is.

## Personal Accountability

Personal accountability is the next important lesson. If you have built a good Team, you are expected, as are the rest of the members, to be of the highest caliber. Hold yourself to these standards as you would anyone else . . . no excuses.

## Real Work

A member of an operational SEAL platoon can figure that about 60 percent of the men on his Team and those around him are experienced SEALs. The rest are new members, affectionately known as "meats." Each platoon's objective is to complete a yearlong workup to prepare for a six-month deployment. And, just like a Team of professionals building through development in their particular specialty, a platoon will participate in several phases of training, learning and honing their skills and tactics in several areas. Each block, or phase, will follow the same basic pattern: Learn, apply, review, evaluate, reapply, reevaluate, and then set SOPs (standard operating procedures).

Getting a job done fast is fruitless if it isn't done right. Individuals and Teams must constantly evaluate their progress. If an individual or Team starts to lose focus, they must take a step back and review.

As a Team member, you can't be afraid to admit that you don't grasp a concept. If the Team is only as fast as its slowest man, you cannot hang in thinking, "I can catch up." You must honestly evaluate your own ability and communicate forthrightly about it—for your own good and for that of the Team. When Team members are unaware of a weak link, they cannot repair it. Unnoticed, the weak link will break, costing time, money, and perhaps even lives.

One block of training for a SEAL platoon is land warfare, which consists of combat tactics and, often, live-fire drills and exercises using live explosives. Particularly dangerous are IADs (immediate action drills), designed to teach a platoon tactics and methods of breaking contact with an enemy force. These involve shooting and moving through different kinds of terrain to evade enemy fire.

In this loud and chaotic environment, the trainers keep the pressure on by setting off explosives to let the Teams know that the enemy is still out there. As the platoon sustains fire, the platoon OIC (officer in charge) looks for a way out. He must, in a matter of seconds, identify and utilize a safe escape route, or the training cadre will start "killing" his men.

The platoon also has the burden of carrying their "dead and wounded" out with them. In addition, each man needs to be aware of the condition of his firearm at all times. When a man gets his turn to jump up and run, he must flick on his safety and be careful not to sweep his buddies with his rifle muzzle, as a hot gun can "cook off" a round at any time. (A cook-off is when the chamber of the gun is hot enough to cause the round sitting in it to combust, inadvertently firing the weapon.) Since everyone is deafened by the noise of gunfire and explosions, each man screams to pass the "word" (instructions) to the next man. This is not the time to play catch-up. When a man doesn't know what's going on or where his people are, he can end up shooting someone or getting shot himself. What's worse is when a man asks someone to explain a concept again, or has to make excuses for why he didn't know where Jim was and why he shot him in the back. When SEALs train with live ordnance, they play for keeps.

In short, what's important to the SEAL Team is important to any Team of professionals in business: Stay informed, stay alert, and stay alive.

## Team Secrets for Innovative Thinking

The unwillingness or inability to think creatively will not only hinder you but will stifle the young and creative untapped innovators in your organization.

Make an anonymous suggestion box available. Let people get rankling details and complaints off their chests. As a Team leader, invite Team members to identify themselves when they drop off suggestions, pointing out that if they do, you can get in touch with them for further discussion.

You may find that most messages are nothing but empty complaints. Stress that no issue will be addressed unless the submitter also includes a viable solution. This will foster an atmosphere of ownership among the Team and innovative and fresh thinking among Team members.

If someone comes to you with a new idea, you must consider it. Barking, "We've done it this way for years and it works fine!" will do nothing but stifle those around you.

From time to time, go to others for their ideas. People like to be challenged. Give them the responsibility and some latitude to be creative for you.

## Be Serious, but Don't Take Yourself So Seriously

Finding the bright side of a bad situation is better than losing your motivation. I can recall several instances when I huddled in a tiny hideout in the woods in miserable conditions. Shaking from the cold and soaking wet, I would turn to my platoon mate and whisper, "Damn, this sucks." He'd reply, "Yeah, but it will make a great story later." If you can find humor in a bad situation and joke about it, you will have a better chance of salvaging your attitude and coming out on top.

## Chapter 1 Lessons

➤ You succeed as a team or fail as a team.

➤ To develop Team skills and to operate accordingly takes time and concerted effort.

➤ Improve the quality of your Team by truly screening your prospective Teammates. This sets the standard from day one.

➤ Accountability is paramount and necessary.

# CHAPTER 2
## *Know Who You've Got*

You must know your Team and what motivates them. If you merely direct day-to-day routine and think of those under you as nameless workers, you are simply "managing." This was well and good forty years ago, when companies demanded marginally educated employees willing to perform the same tasks for eight to ten hours a day. But it is terribly wasteful in an era when higher education, varied skills, and creative abilities are absolutely necessary for success—both for the individual and for the business. This applies to civilian as well as military ranks. The modern workplace does not need mere managers; it needs leaders who will continually develop those entrusted to their care. It is important to practice sound management tactics to ensure the stability of your business, but it is also crucial that you expand your leadership skills to ensure that your Team members succeed as well.

Of the men who graduated BUD/S with me, most were enlisted. Sixty percent of them had bachelor's or associate's degrees, and at least two had master's. One of my classmates had been an electrical engineer for Westinghouse for several years before joining the service. The more you learn about your Team members, the more you will be amazed by the vast pool of knowledge you have to draw from. Review résumés, ask questions, and get to know those you work with. The time you spend learning about your people will yield information that could prove valuable in the future.

Aside from the fact that individual Team members will know that you are interested in their success and welfare, you will gain a greater understanding of how to best utilize each individual in your Team—which will benefit not only the Team as a whole but also each individual. Each SEAL platoon has "departments" to manage the gear required for the many aspects of SEAL missions. The ordnance department handles all issues dealing with bullets, bombs, and weapons. The communications department handles all radios, computers, and ancillary communications equipment. The air department manages parachutes and rigging and preparation of equipment involved in air operations. Diving maintains and repairs open- and closed-circuit diving gear and logistics concerning submerged operations. Intelligence handles information, maps, and cameras. The engineering department handles the Zodiac boats, motors, and other assorted hardware. The two corpsmen make up the platoon's medical department.

With so many jobs requiring time and specific expertise, it is in the Team's best interest to assign to each department those best able to handle the tasks involved. I have a passion for parachuting and aviation, so I was sent to rigger school, jumpmaster school, and other air operations–oriented schools. I headed up the air operations department. Invariably, every platoon is going to have a "motorhead," to whom you'll want to entrust your engines. The last thing you need ten miles offshore are piles of useless metal that were formerly engines. Every SEAL carries and is responsible for a weapon. But when it comes to collateral duties, such as those a specific department handles for the good of the Team, platoon commanders do what they can to accommodate the interests of each individual SEAL. Platoon riggers are highly trained and are the only men allowed to pack reserve parachutes. To my way of thinking, it would be awfully nice if the rigger actually enjoyed his job.

People will look up to you simply because of your position and the aura of responsibility associated with your title. Removing yourself from your Team and planning you next career step will only serve to alienate and blind you. While absorbed in seeking your own selfish goals, you will not be in tune with your Team.

Get involved and experience the wide-eyed enthusiasm that will greet you when your Team members realize you are involved in and concerned about their well-being and future. I am not suggesting that you invite them to your house every weekend to play with your dog and eat hamburgers. But you must make it evident that one of your duties—which you sincerely and willfully undertake—is Team custodian. This entails the general maintenance and care of the Team—as well as the "cleaning out" of unsuitable members, if need be!

You will be a revered and effective leader if you take the time to find out what drives each member to succeed. With this knowledge, you can assign your people to tasks and missions more efficiently and with the greatest good of the Team in mind. No matter how you hold it to the light, personnel are the Team's greatest assets—and yours individually. Identify those members with a propensity or knack for future assignments or projects. You may have two people who don't like what they are doing and would be thrilled to switch. This simple knowledge can allow you to make the change and produce a stronger, more effective Team.

Before SEALs go into the field for an operation, the Team is evaluated to ensure the optimum placement of personnel. The officer in charge knows exactly who is going on the mission, what their specialties are, and what roles they will fill. Take a good look at your Team. You need to scrutinize each person and identify his or her strengths and weaknesses—always with the good of the Team, and the individual, in mind.

As a leadership tool, maintain a small file on each member of the Team. Be open about what you are doing and make clear to your Team that you will be using the information in the file to perform periodic evaluations. You must set standardized evaluation parameters and continually refine your evaluation system to make it bias free. Use evaluation sheets to track positive and negative performances.

In the SEALs, the evaluation file is a great tool for leaders, as they rate individual performance against a Navy standard. This helps selection boards make better decisions about individual advancement. Within the platoon, the chief maintains a "training jacket" on all the members of the Team. This file usually contains, but is not limited to, information about the individual's advancement and performance in specific training and professional development schools. It also contains periodic evaluations and lists the sailor's special qualifications. Further evaluations track outstanding performance and document trends in substandard performance. The latter is crucial if a member proves to be a safety hazard or is just not suited for the job and must be removed. In order to sustain the high quality and integrity of your Team, you must maintain a set schedule for reviews and ensure that the evaluation process is executed without bias. You can use an unbiased periodic and active evaluation system to terminate those who poison the Team or who don't have Team goals in mind.

Often people hesitate to document poor performance because the subject of the evaluation is "a nice person" or has convinced the reviewer that their future performance will be better. But what should have been the final straw cannot be the first time you document performance issues. That hurts the individual, who did not have the proper impetus to improve their performance or competence, and the organization and the people in it, who must suffer through this potentially dangerous fumbling, followed by the pain of termination or even a lawsuit.

It's also crucial that your evaluation process be objective and detailed enough to be fair to the individuals concerned, in the event that someone other than you needs to utilize the information. Fair and objective evaluation and documentation will also allow the next leader to do what is best for their Team and the individuals in it.

Moreover, if your Team knows what you are doing and why, as you undertake an evaluation and documentation regimen, there will be no surprises. Each member will know that you are serious, and that you are willing to take action in the best interest of the whole.

You must be able to distinguish the difference between a good person and a good operator. In the SEAL community, some men must be let go in the best interest of the Team. The sailor who is not working in the Team may be a nice person, tops. But he may not be appropriate for the job.

If a member of the Team just doesn't grasp the finer points of the job, it can cost your organization a lot of money. It can cause extra work and irritation for other Team members, particularly if the person in question suffers from chronic incompetence, for whatever reason. In the SEAL Teams this person could eventually cost himself or another his life in a training exercise or on a real-world mission. Constant evaluation can tell you whether you can afford to work with a "leadership challenge" or whether it makes more sense to find a replacement. The Team has to come first!

To put this another way, you must consider the possible moral issue of keeping a nonperformer. You should track chronic poor performance and take action—even if that means termination—if the situation does not improve over a reasonable period of time. Action, as painful as it can be, will prove to your Team that you are dedicated to the quality of its members and its product or service, and that you will act to preserve the integrity and safety of the Team. Consider the ramifications of allowing a substandard performer to remain a part of your Team. The dedicated members will eventually become fed up and lose faith in your ability to protect the Team. What would be your perception of a leader who you knew had prior knowledge of a personnel issue but was unwilling to rectify the situation? If the weak Team member is truly a good person, try to find another job for them. Do not keep them on for fear of hurting their feelings. It will hurt both them and your Team. Sloth and apathy breed rapidly, and if other Team members see that a low level of performance is accepted by the Team leadership, they will have difficulty producing a high-quality product or service and may soon adopt easier, if inferior, standards.

There was a sailor in my sister platoon who had a problem with situational awareness in the "kill house," a building in which SEALs practice in-house shooting with live ammunition. This is an extremely dangerous exercise, since you are shooting real bullets in close quarters. The sailor in question repeatedly shot his rifle inches from the faces of his Teammates. Other than this, he was a great person and an extremely hard worker, always one of the last to leave work, always willing to lend a hand to anyone in need. But in the special-warfare business, you cannot afford to be bad at anything. This sailor was given several opportunities to enhance his awareness. After he proved that he was unable to maintain the proper awareness in the kill house, he lost his SEAL qualification and was transferred from the Team. Although it was hard to see a good man taken down a notch, it did not make sense to wait until someone's parents had to be informed that their son was dead because we didn't want to hurt another sailor's feelings.

The Navy has long selected its finest enlisted personnel to become officers. Choosing officer candidates from the ranks offers several advantages over outside recruitment. First and foremost, the organization has its choice from a pool of personnel who have already made a commitment to the service. They know the organization and have chosen to stay. They are not coming to the Navy green, unsure of what to expect. This is not to say that there are not many advantages to getting a fresh outlook and new ideas from outsiders. However, those already part of the Team know what they are getting into. These people know, for the most part, how the organization works. Perhaps the greatest advantage to choosing from existing personnel is access to documentation of their performance according to Navy standards; the Navy's great leadership tool, the periodic, standardized evaluation, provides selection Teams with a method to evaluate the potential and worth of advancement candidates.

At a certain point early in my career, I was building an application package. The Team was about to have a change of command, and I had spoken at length with the outgoing commanding officer about the prospects of a commission. But my package was not going to be complete before he left. The commander assured me that he would brief the incoming C.O. about my record and my desire for a commission. He did not endorse my selection, as the new C.O. would be making the decision, but he did recommend me for the commission. Two other men from the Team also applied for the same program.

Although we would compete against applicants drawn from the entire Navy, the C.O. ranked our packages against one another. Two of us were to deploy on a mission in two weeks, and the commission packages were due in Pensacola in three. Preparations for deployment are quite extensive and time consuming, and there are family matters to tend to because of the upcoming six-month absence. The new C.O. interviewed the three of us for about fifteen minutes each. Then we left our application packages with the administration department, to be completed and sent to us later, since the new C.O. had not yet made a decision regarding endorsement of any of the candidates.

Once we were overseas, I called my Team to make sure my package had been sent. To my dismay, the new C.O. had not endorsed any of the officer-candidate packages. The next day the C.O. called to explain that he felt I was a great SEAL but did not yet have enough experience to be a successful officer candidate. With all the diplomacy I could muster, I stated that I was very qualified, in fact, an excellent candidate, and that I was competing against fleet sailors without half the qualifications. He agreed and then gave me his take. I remember gripping the phone with white knuckles as he spoke.

"I know you are an outstanding sailor," he told me, "and will make a great officer, but you are a *SEAL under my command*. If I am going to put you in for a commission, you are not going to be the best compared to the rest of the Navy, you are going to be the best compared to you! If you want to be a naval officer, I want more! I want you to show me that you are ready while you are on this deployment. When you get back to the States, I want you to become a static line jumpmaster and a range safety officer. I want you to take on more responsibility."

I was furious. I did, however, have one of the best workouts in a long time after that phone call! Later, one of the officers in my platoon helped me understand the C.O.'s viewpoint and the responsibility inherent in recommending someone for a commission. This was a lesson in personnel management and responsibility I shall never forget.

On returning home, I requested both static line jumpmaster and range safety officer (RSO) school and completed the training as soon as I came back from postdeployment leave. Afterward, I moved into the Team's "training cell," which was responsible for preparing SEAL platoons for deployment. A month after RSO school, I was in the desert preparing a training scenario for a night exercise. The C.O. would be coming to observe, but I was still bitter and not particularly excited to see him. The C.O. arrived and watched us complete the setup. As we walked away to await the platoon's arrival, he caught up to me.

He started off by saying, "I recently signed two qualifications letters with your name on them. The word is that you kicked ass in that last platoon. You did everything I asked of you, and I was wondering if you are still interested in a commission."

After I explained that I had already started putting another package together, he said he would do everything he could to ensure its success.

At that point everything was clear. This man was a true leader and a man of integrity. He hadn't just looked at my qualifications to judge me; he'd tested me to "know" me. What made me tick? Did I have that extra ounce of resolve necessary to be a naval officer?

Another insight I gleaned from the experience was that we must be the custodians of our Team. Being a Team member means being aggressively proactive. Take ownership and pride in the Team. Encourage each and every member of the Team to evaluate every situation. You cannot rely on "someone else" to screen and evaluate your Team for you.

This does not mean that you should head-hunt or nitpick. Rather, stay alert for potential problems and stop them as soon as they appear. Know your people. Promote by experience and not by paper. Test, evaluate, and judge.

Promotion should not be simply a function of time or checked boxes. Looking back, I wish more C.O.s had the morals, standards, and resolve mine did when it came to deciding whether to endorse my officer-candidate package. If you are involved in the promotion process, you will be judged by the quality of those you promote.

## Chapter 2 Lessons

➤ Stay involved. How can you learn about your Team if you are aloof and distant?

➤ Assets. Learn to identify and utilize the talents of those on your Team. Satisfied people are happy people.

➤ When considering the fate of one, consider the well-being of all.

➤ Document issues. If it is worth your time to deal with, document it. A thorough and appropriate paper trail can save your butt.

➤ Identify potential problems before they become critical.

➤ When you take charge, you become entrusted with and responsible for the welfare and morale of the Team.

➤ Being a nice person is not a job qualification. Know who your Team members are, what they are interested in, and what they do best.

➤ Challenge your Team. Break up day-to-day monotony by pushing individual Team members to develop themselves.

➤ Be the custodian of your Team and encourage others to accept the same responsibility.

➤ Know and develop; know and remove.

# CHAPTER 3

## *Setting the Stage*

### Challenge your Team—mediocrity is boring, unchallenging, and, ultimately, demoralizing.

As a leader, you must be accountable for the development and direction of your Team. *Team* is a dynamic term. Freedom is important and should be granted to all, but if you do not provide direction and stability, the framework and foundation of the Team will falter and crumble. You must provide your Team with the tools and bearing necessary for every individual to make the right decisions, be successful, and develop their future subordinates. You must all think long-term and prepare the path for solid values now.

You, as a leader, must set the stage by making perfectly clear what you expect of the Team and every individual in it. Even if you are already part of a Team, or have recently joined one, you can still set the stage. It requires effort and time to implement any plan, regardless of your resolve, with an existing Team. There must be no gray area in the goals and standards you establish. As the business environment changes, your Team's goals must change and improve, but they must always be clear. Set standards high and be honest and open about what they are and how to achieve them. People want to be accepted, and when excellence is the norm, they will perform at that level to be part of the Team.

Let individual Team members know your plan and vision for the Team and encourage involvement. It will require the efforts of all to accomplish Team goals, so keep everyone in the loop. Call it a vision, mission statement, dream, Team goal—whatever you want; just make sure that your vision for the Team encompasses aspects of your personal leadership plan as well as your Team's direction and goals. What begins as the simple need for companionship will soon develop into a solid work ethic. After setting goals for the Team, let every individual on the Team know what you expect and demand from them. Make it clear what will happen if Team principles and individual goals are not met. By the same token, praise your Team for good work.

Hundreds of men want to be part of the SEAL Team. Only those who perform at the highest levels achieve the goal. Those unwilling or unable to make the grade or perform as a Team member are released without regret. When you are a proactive leader and part of the best Team around, you will always have a vast pool of interested hard chargers to screen. Be that leader and be that Team!

## Accountability

Accountability is a central working principle of the Team. As a SEAL, when you are culpable for a wrongdoing, you own up to it and face the consequences. Among the ranks of the Naval Special Warfare community, it is incomparably worse to be known as seedy and deceitful than to have done wrong and admitted it. Those who are unwilling to accept responsibility for their actions are frowned upon and find themselves either remediated or removed.

Loss of trust and confidence kills a Team and cannot be tolerated. Detect, document, and do away with it. There is neither time nor room for ownerless error in the SEALs or in any Team. Deal with situations swiftly and appropriately. Be fair, thorough, and effective in doling out consequences for poor performance and deceitful behavior.

It is futile to encourage and expect people to do the right thing when they know they can get by with mediocre performance. It is crucial that you make clear that accountability is not only proper but expected, and that anything else is unacceptable and intolerable.

Unless you hold your Team to a high standard, you will receive substandard work, often based on unclear goals, weak discipline, and muddy thinking. When the time comes, you must not hesitate to follow through with your plan. Part of setting the stage is carrying out your warnings about the results of indiscretion on the part of one of your people. Failure to do so will undermine your future endeavors and attempts to maintain control of your Team. You will lose that valuable edge required to lead, for you will no longer be holding yourself accountable.

If you fail to hold those who do not perform to your standard responsible, your Team will disintegrate. You will cultivate the perception that you are spineless and unwilling to make the necessary, if difficult, decisions.

## Ownership

As a SEAL, when you are on an exercise or operation, all you have is your gear and your Team. If you take care of your gear, it will take care of you! Instill a sense of ownership of your mission and the equipment you will use to accomplish it. People will be more ambitious and take better care of their tools when they perceive that they own a piece of what they are to do.

SEAL Teams have a decent budget that allows for the purchase of good, serviceable gear. But just because we have the resources doesn't mean that we can treat our gear as disposable. We follow a hierarchy of importance: *Team gear, my gear, me!* This is an unwritten law.

When we finish any exercise, our first duty is to take care of the Team, or "common," gear. We clean and stow the boats, motors, trucks, parachutes, and any other gear specific to that mission. Two men in each platoon are designated as custodians of each of the various types of gear. This does not mean that they clean and repair it by themselves. Rather, when that type of gear sees use, they take the helm and direct the rest of the platoon in the care and maintenance of it. If we all use it, we all clean it.

Once the common gear is cared for, we tend to our personal gear: weapons, radios, load-bearing equipment, and dive gear. All is made ready for the next evolution. Only then do we hit the showers. On rare occasions, some SEALs choose to break this chain. The other men make the transgressors well aware of their indiscretion, and usually those in error wind up having to buy the rest of the platoon a case of beer. After a training exercise, we always get everybody's input and take note of the lessons learned. We usually put on comfortable clothes and grab something to eat to give the debriefing a more relaxed and productive atmosphere.

I remember the first time I stood in formation on the beach in Coronado, California, ready for a swimmer inspection by the staff. These inspections happen before every swim as a safety measure, to ensure that all the students have properly working safety equipment. The most important points of the inspection are the carbon dioxide–actuated life vest and fixed-blade knife all SEALs carry. Salt air and seawater wreak havoc on metal and material, and since SEALs are always in the water while in BUD/S, the cleaning and maintenance of all gear is a daily event. That day, the entire class was lined up on the beach, geared up for the weekly two-mile timed swim. Two lines of men faced each other, each man standing across from his swim buddy. All wore a wet suit top and hood, UDT (Underwater Demolition Team) shorts, a pistol belt with a flare and knife sheath, dive booties, and a UDT life vest with a dive mask stuffed inside it. Each man's fins stood tepeed next to him, heel cups wedged together and the blades dug into the sand.

A length of thin orange line attached my mask to my vest, to avoid the possible loss of it in the surf zone. My nose filled with the heavy salt air, and I felt the boom of the crashing waves in my chest. The first instructor to arrive, the corpsman, raced up in the ambulance, a 4x4 Suburban designed to handle the soft beach sand. One student, the class leading petty officer (LPO), yelled, *"Instructor Smith!"* and the entire class responded with, *"Hoo-yah, Instructor Smith!"* This ritual was repeated as each new instructor arrived. The instructors descended on the students, looking for any faults. As they pored over our gear, the instructor in the ambulance fired up the public address system and asked if anyone wanted to quit. In a monotone voice he said, "You can make the pain stop. Just come over to the ambulance, and I'll give you a warm blanket and a cup of hot cocoa. You don't have to do this. I will help you find your niche in the Navy."

With devious smiles, the other instructors searched our eyes for doubt. They always tried to make us question our ability to pass the pending swim. "Is that all you guys are wearing? That water is cold, I sure hope you don't hype out," one would say, referring to the very real danger of hypothermia. "I hope we picked the right time to coincide with the tide and currents," another might mention, "or at least half the class will fail."

One of our duties was to provide the instructors with a surf-observation report. It was a drill to help us learn how to read the ocean. At times they would let us pick the direction of the swim, and then we had to have faith in the men who had prepared the report that day, because their mistake could cause the entire class to fail.

The formal inspection started, students standing at attention with both hands out, arms bent at the elbow. In my right hand I held the carbon dioxide cartridge for the UDT vest and in the left my perfectly sharp knife. The instructors examined every inch of my gear to see that I had properly maintained it. If they had found corroded areas, tears, or any signs that I had not taken care of my gear, it would have been time to "pay the man." Punishment takes many forms. A favorite is flutter kicks or push-ups until the instructor gets tired of counting. One of the worst involves doing these exercises in the surf, known as getting "wet and sandy" or turning into a "sugar cookie." The packed sand in your shorts and wet suit will cause painful chafing during the ensuing swim.

Some of the instructors had bald spots on their arms where they had tested the edges of countless knives. Keeping knives sharp in Coronado is a difficult task because the salt air and water continuously corrode and deteriorate the edges. That day, one of the instructors became furious because he was finding dull knives. He picked up a rock and yelled, "Okay, gents, if you don't want to sharpen your knives, I will do it for you!" From that point forward, every time he found a less than razor-sharp knife, he smashed the rock on the blade until the blade was flat. The additional hours it took those students to fix the flat blades or procure new knives to replace the broken ones was enough to convince the entire class that the extra few minutes to hone their knife edges perfectly was well worth the time.

## Team Concept

I will use the swim to further illustrate the importance of accountability. At BUD/S, all SEALs must meet certain standards. If the time to beat is thirty minutes, then thirty minutes and one second is failing. After each swim the time for each individual is posted. The failure column frequently lists times mere seconds off the prescribed time. You may be saying to yourself that if someone was only one second off, they should pass; maybe the timing instructor was slow to hit the stopwatch. Maybe. But the standards were fully explained and posted, and if Team members are worried about how fast the instructor moves his thumb, they should swim faster!

During these trying ordeals each man must also rely on his buddy. If one fails, so does the other. Individuals in pairs are not allowed to stray more than six feet from their partners. From day one in Naval Special Warfare, the most important rule is "Never leave your buddy." If the instructors do find a man more than six feet away from his buddy on a swim, he soon finds himself tethered to his partner. The pair must then carry out all their daily activities attached to each other with a six-foot section of mooring line. This burden is designed to impress upon the Team members the importance of working with partners and never leaving someone behind. Not only is leaving a buddy a safety hazard during open-ocean swims, but it also goes against all that SEALs hold sacred.

Teamwork comes into play in almost every SEAL exercise. If someone's swim buddy is having an off day, the prepared man, or the one who is at a higher level of conditioning or mental readiness, does not have the option of leaving his partner behind and swimming ahead to make sure that he passes the test. The pair passes or fails together. It is each man's responsibility to provide his Teammate with the motivation he needs to pass the time trial. I have seen men drag their buddies through the water to make sure the pair meets the swim time. Every man dares to take it upon himself to do whatever he can to ensure the success of his Teammates—not only because he might be the one having trouble next time, but also because it is the right thing to do.

In Second Phase, diving phase, the pair concept is taken to another level. Diving operations are inherently dangerous. When you couple this with the clandestine duties of a Frogman, you stack the odds in favor of mishap. That is why SEALs must be physically and mentally conditioned at all times. Every event dealing with dive operations, as well as all others, is handled as the life-and-death matter it is.

When diving with rebreather dive rigs, which use 100 percent oxygen, are completely closed, and do not expel bubbles, the chance of a casualty increases. Although this equipment can be fatal if the operators lose their situational awareness, it is the most clandestine diving equipment available.

The first portion of Second Phase is devoted to educating future SEALs about the proper handling of equipment and the signs of danger for diving operations. In most cases a man and his buddy will have mere seconds to take lifesaving action once signs are recognized. The instructor staff goes to great lengths to impress upon Team members the magnitude of Teamwork while working underwater at night with no light. Deviation from the Naval Special Warfare's strict diving regulations is grounds for immediate dismissal from the program.

There is nothing more detestable than someone who leaves a Teammate in need. This doesn't mean that the strong should coddle the weak and carry them from day to day. Those who are not up to snuff must either be brought up to standard or let go.

If you have anyone in your organization willing to walk away from a Teammate in need, "impress" upon them the necessity to change this attitude. If the individual in question is unwilling to adopt the Team spirit, cut them and their gangrenous attitude from your Team immediately. Make sure that being a Team player is part of your mission statement and evaluation system. Such individuals are not tolerated on the SEAL Teams. They should not be on yours.

There are, however, certain circumstances when individual effort receives reward, such as timed runs, either flat or through the obstacle courses. Then the men who finish early run back to encourage those who have not yet finished. Non-Team players are reminded of their indiscretion during Team evolutions. For individuals unwilling to participate as Team members, BUD/S instructors have devised a wonderful remedy. They have the individual lounge on the beach as if on vacation as the staff "hammers" the rest of the class in front of them. Usually within minutes, that person is begging to rejoin the class. To add insult to injury, the lounging classmate is given the bullhorn and made to "hammer" the class himself. After about half an hour of this, the Team either has a devout Teammate or one less person.

## Chapter 3 Lessons

➤ Define these principles briefly, writing a one-sentence summary for each one:

➤ Accountability.

➤ Ownership.

➤ Team gear, my gear, me!

➤ Team concept.

➤ No ambiguity in mission statement.

➤ Challenge the Team with high standards.

# CHAPTER 4
## *The Pragmatic Pedestal*

The confident, self-assured leader is the "quiet professional." These people lead by example and establish credibility by virtue of their own nature. They are positive role models, the kind of people the ranks want to emulate. As a leader your position and power will be greater than that of your Teammates but must be realistic.

Regardless of age, race, or gender, the confident, quiet professional is much more effective and respected than the arrogant figurehead. A bullish and tyrannical businessman may be professionally savvy but is rarely a good leader—and is often an ostentatious blowhard. *Businessman* is singular. *Leader* connotes the presence of a Team. Arrogance is not a positive leadership quality. One who attempts to establish credibility by demeaning others only undermines the goals he or she hopes to accomplish. Such a person also chips away at the chain of command and stifles a Team that might otherwise achieve great things. Arrogance in the leadership corps serves only to cultivate the type of working environment that is consumed by mistrust and malice, contempt and fear. In this environment, coworkers compete for survival, hoping that they will not be the next to go. This type of competition is nonproductive and unhealthy. It is impossible for people to concentrate fully on their work when they dread the presence of the "boss" or the bad intent of their coworkers.

Professionals and businesspeople tend to believe that they need to look out only for themselves and not worry about anyone else. They struggle to set themselves apart. Relentless in pursuit of their goals, they perform for themselves at the expense of others.

That's no way to build a Team. The Team must work together efficiently toward the success of all Team members—through the success of the Team as one unit. Conceit and self-righteousness have no place. If allowed to exist, these shortcomings will cause the Team to fail.

In a SEAL Team, if any man has a problem, the commanding officer wants to know about it. The chain of command must handle the problem at the lowest level possible, but he wants to know the status of his Team members so he can make the right decisions for the good of the Team. Every SEAL, regardless of rank, recognizes the importance of knowing not only whom you've got but what is going on with every part of the Team.

A leader who places himself above the Team may get a bird's-eye view of the floor plan but will have little knowledge of the situation there. Once or twice a year, and more often if necessary, the commanding officer of a SEAL Team holds something called a "captain's call." This Team meeting provides an opportunity for any Team member to have the C.O.'s ear on any situation or subject he feels inclined to speak about. The C.O. reserves the right to redirect the question to another Team member better suited to handle the situation. But he specifically allots time in his unrelentingly busy schedule to listen to every member of his Team and address their concerns. Commanding officers who use this tool effectively enjoy the efforts of a supported and motivated Team.

Through this process they are able to keep their fingers on the pulse of the Team and are more fully equipped and better informed to handle both current and potential issues.

The most effective officers have learned to manage the relationship between seniors and subordinates. This delicate balance depends largely on the maturity and personality of the Team and its members. If you are in a position of authority, those around you do not need to be reminded of this on a daily basis. Confident and consistent leadership negates the need to reaffirm your position overtly—show, don't tell. The archetypal special-warfare officer earns respect because he is a staunch protector of his men and not a self-absorbed weasel.

Team leadership has a shelf life. Retrofit your Team's power and authority structure with distinct, unique, and dynamic leadership tactics. You don't need to spend eight months in the mountains seeking divine enlightenment to develop these tactics, and they don't need to be implemented overnight. Personal leadership's flexibility allows you to adapt to any number of work environments and situations. This is your venue for expressing your personality and humanity. Do not become complacent. Never stop developing yourself or your Team!

Among motivated professionals there will always be a natural competitiveness. You have to set the stage for excellence. The entire Team knows what to expect from you and what they should demand from one another. Arrogance sets the Team leader up for failure. Before long, even the most dedicated and open-minded employees will yearn to see the haughty boss fall flat on his or her face.

It is a rank misconception that the driven, egotistic boss is productive. While work may get done, this style of leadership has long-term detrimental effects on the Team, the business, and the organization. When you are a part of your Team, and your Team truly supports you, the foundation for success is solid. Do not think too highly of yourself. Be a leader. Let others think highly of you, and let them place you in high regard!

So, as the boss, how important are you? You are in charge, and with that power you have the ability to influence others both within and outside the workplace. This is not to be taken lightly. Your decisions and how you handle situations will reach far beyond the confines of the workplace. That all Team members leave domestic matters at home is neither realistic nor possible; home and work are intertwined. To properly deal with a problem, you might have to adversely affect the personal lives of some of your Team members. But if you become callous and ambivalent toward the personal interests and well-being of your Team, you will soon find that you don't have one. Your cutthroat attitude will create in your Team members a perception that you are arrogant. When this happens, you will lose credibility and trust. A chain of command is designed to handle issues, but Team members must know that they can approach you if they need to, and they must be comfortable doing so. Be involved and be successful.

Those who have shown a willingness to use the misfortune of others to get ahead in the SEAL Teams quickly find themselves isolated and distrusted. While this is disturbing for the individual, it also breaks a Team down. Soon everyone is watching his back and those of his buddies and losing concentration on the task at hand. These poisonous non-Team players must quickly be removed from the ranks—to preserve the Team and to keep it efficient and successful in its mission and a safe haven for all the remaining members.

If you know you have a propensity to think only of yourself, fix it now! Don't be "the one" who secures personal remuneration as a result of selfish manipulation of the Team.

As a Team leader, you need to analyze your leadership tactics and determine whether the power and influence you enjoy have been earned or merely hijacked by the authority granted your position. "Rank has its privileges," we say in the Navy. And it should. You have put in a lot of time and energy. You have earned the rewards, respect, rights, and privileges of being a member of the hierarchy. At the same time, you must accept the increasing responsibility that comes with your achievements. To be an effective leader, you must relish the added responsibility and work as opportunities arise to help your people become successes in their own right.

Being a leader is a privilege, not a right. If you realize this and act accordingly, you will improve the overall character of the work environment. If this isn't your philosophy, then you are in it for the wrong reasons; you must rethink your agenda or you will have a lonely, brief, and unsuccessful stay at the top. Stick with the tried and true, but never stop looking for ways to improve your leadership and the business you and your Team conduct.

Without your Team, you are just a person in charge. You may think you are at the top of the heap, kicking butt, and taking names. Imagine, however, how much more effective you will be when you work for the best interests of each of your people. If you make it evident that you hold your Team members' advancement and personal and professional interests in high regard, you will find that they will become increasingly loyal and more willing to give you all their energy.

During my time in Naval Special Warfare I have worked with men who had the Team concept running through their veins. I'll call one of the men who made the greatest impact on me "Chief." Chief began his naval career in the lowest enlisted pay grade and worked his way up to earn a commission as a warrant officer. I worked with him when he was the leading chief petty officer of my second platoon.

Chief is an up-front, trustworthy, and reliable leader. He has never flaunted or abused his fortune. You always know where he stands and what he expects. It is always clear that his first priority is his men and their needs, whether personal or professional. He is a busy man, yet he is also the first to lend a hand to the junior men. He wants to make sure each man in his command receives proper training, development, and guidance. The result is that Chief is an extremely credible leader whose ethics span his entire life. I know many successful Team members who attribute their good fortune to his mentorship.

When Chief becomes visibly angry, people move. When he couples that with an order, people move even faster. He so seldom gets angry— and even more rarely expresses it outwardly—because he has built solid respect and a healthy work environment. He does not separate himself from the Team, and he is a working member and mentor. Everyone wants to keep him happy because it seems indecent to perform at any lower level.

Chief is a man I would follow anywhere and without a second of hesitation because I know he holds in high regard my best interest and that of the Team. His men understand that any task he assigns that may be high-risk or result in bodily harm will work out for the greater benefit of the Team. My respect for him is such that if he chooses me to sacrifice for the Team, I will do so gladly with the knowledge that what I am doing has to be done and requires my skills.

As a sign of solidarity and common decency, great leaders will, at times, forgo some of the accoutrements afforded them. If you have been fortunate enough to avoid beginning at the bottom, you must understand how important it is for your Team to know that their leader is concerned about their well-being. If you want an effective Team and greater success, you must make the effort to learn, understand, or experience what each Team member has gone through to get where they are, as well as what they go through in their present position. You will be amazed at the work ethic and productivity of a fully incorporated Team.

I had one commanding officer who would don his combat gear whenever possible and participate in training exercises with his men. Although his duties as C.O. of a SEAL Team did not call for him to participate in training, he took the time and effort to stay sharp and involved with the Team. He believed, as well, that his men could feed him status reports all day long, but unless he actually got in the mix, he would never truly gauge the climate. This man enjoyed unparalleled respect from his men for his continuous efforts to be part of the Team, not merely the figurehead on top. Even though he's no longer in the service, stories are still told of his charisma and strikingly effective leadership.

If you started in the lower ranks, congratulations on your success and advancement. But you should know that you will lose or fail to gain respect unless you always remember where you came from. Promotion must never be about revenge. I was selected from the enlisted ranks for a commission. After checking out of my SEAL Team, I arrived in Newport, Rhode Island, for a two-month indoctrination into the officer corps. I was the only SEAL out of the eighty sailors in my class. I had high hopes and expected that I would be working with highly motivated, like-minded personnel who were as dedicated to the Navy and the custody of the enlisted ranks as I was. My vision of being an exceptional officer included the protection, development, and betterment of the enlisted corps, as well as a vigilant assessment of the officer corps.

During our first week in Newport we reported to the uniform shop for our new officer uniforms. It was a great day for me—after nearly ten years of naval service, my dream of earning a commission was close at hand. Similar pride was evident in the faces and actions of my new Teammates as they donned their new uniforms and stood tall for the tailor. Then I heard an utterance that depressed me. "I can't wait to get commissioned and get back to the fleet," a man behind me said. "I can't wait until Jack sees who is really in charge—I'll show him."

I turned to the man and said, "If that's why you're here, do us all a favor and get the hell out of here now!" If it were up to me, I would have discharged that guy right there. His sort of self-righteous attitude can only poison and destroy a Team. This man had been part of the program for only a week and already he planned to set himself above everyone else and abuse his power and position.

You must remain steadfast and true to solid leadership principles while being flexible enough to adapt to a wide range of situations without compromising your integrity or the sanctity of your Team. Being a leader takes time and effort, and your capabilities will grow as you progress. You can be satisfied with your current model of tactics as long as you do not allow yourself to become complacent and taciturn in the pursuit of improvement. Keep a constant vigil on how you present yourself. Perception is reality, and your Team can perceive only what they see. Absence begets suspicion; that is why it is so imperative to be involved and visible. Leadership should be fun and fulfilling, so enjoy it—but not at the expense of your Team.

## Chapter 4 Lessons

➤ Do not think too highly of yourself; let others do that for you.

➤ Enjoy your success; you earned it. But beware of overindulgence.

➤ Don't forget where you came from if you were once in the trenches. Remain cognizant of the needs of those who are still there.

➤ If you started on top, do not spend your time patting yourself on the back—that is a waste of valuable time that could be spent developing your subordinates. Create the opportunity to learn the inner workings of your Team. How can you expect to efficiently run a machine if you don't know how it works?

➤ Have confidence: Be strong, be real, and be trusted.

➤ Say what needs to be said. If you sugarcoat your thoughts, your message will be lost.

➤ Absence begets suspicion.

# CHAPTER 5
## *Have an Open-Door Policy for Opportunity*

The way your Team perceives you is reality. Leadership is action. It is as dynamic as a shoreline that is pummeled by the surf and carved by the tides. Your leadership style must develop and improve. Once you settle on what you think is right or become unwilling or too apathetic to notice the need for change, you become a run-of-the-mill manager. But if you really want to make a difference, challenge yourself and your Team. Your leadership style may already work—and it is important to recognize and use what works. Just make sure that you maintain a constant vigilance and are willing to change things when necessary.

Some people have an innate ability to lead. But it is entirely possible to learn, practice, and develop the skills required to become an outstanding leader. It is important to read widely on the topic, observe the leadership styles of others, and ask questions of those you admire and regard as great leaders. If they are worth your admiration, they will most certainly make time to speak with you and help you develop your own tactics.

Your leadership style must be your own. This is not to say that you can't or shouldn't emulate great leaders, but you must add your own personal touch. This is the root of respect and a firm basis on which to build your reputation as an innovative and well-versed leader. You should be sound and solid in your approach but have enough of your own personality woven into the blanket of protection for your Team, because that blanket is your leadership. This is the opportunity you have to share *your* personality with your Team on a professional level.

One of the fastest ways to develop resentment in your Team is to be a "do as I say" leader. Are you always heard and never seen? Do you hold your Team to standards you are not willing to abide by yourself?

You must assess your actions from the vantage point of your personnel and that of your peers. How would you perceive those actions if undertaken by anyone else? Honest introspection is a powerful tool that has helped me immensely over the years. If your Team acts or reacts uncharacteristically in a situation, before you accuse them of impropriety, examine your recent actions. This might—and often does—solve the mystery. Your every action and this inventory taking must be about the Team! Those who believe in their Teams and are part of them lead great Teams. An outwardly positive and cooperative attitude is infectious. A leader who exemplifies this Team spirit will soon find that he has a group that is united, is interested in success, and can virtually run itself.

Team members expect and need consistency from their leader. They must know what to expect, and if drastic change is on the way, they need time to prepare for the discomfort. If those in your care think *Team* is merely a term you use to bolster their spirits, they will be apt to treat it accordingly. They may even ignore you when you need them to overcome adversity and pull together.

One of the main reasons SEAL Teams are so successful is that a close bond exists between the officers and the men. All endure the same training and have a common experience. The officers would never ask the men to do something they would not be willing or able to do themselves. A platoon OIC (officer in charge) shouldn't have to participate in every task in daily platoon life; he has got plenty of work to keep him busy. But he must remain cognizant of the situations his men face and be able to give them direction—and so must you. Think about what you are going to ask your Team to do. Does it make sense? How would you react if you were in their shoes? If the task or tasks seem outlandish and ridiculous, are there other alternatives or solutions?

Avoid the knee-jerk-reaction approaches to problem solving. Consult, cooperate, correct! There will be many times when this luxury is elusive. But when you have the opportunity to deliberate and go over solutions with your people, helping them to come to solutions themselves, take it.

Often SEAL Teams do not have the time to consider all the options. Decisions need to be made immediately, based on the information at hand. A mediocre decision now is better than the best decision made too late. In these moments, your track record with your Team will either hinder or strengthen your authority. If you have a reputation for being dynamic, flexible, fair, and wise, your Team will take the rough spots in stride and back you until the job is completed.

On the other hand, if you are known or perceived to be apathetic, arrogant, aloof, or self-righteous, you will very likely be given only the bare minimum. Your personnel will put forth enough effort to maintain a paycheck as they look for a more fruitful working environment elsewhere. If you have employees who are satisfied with a repressive atmosphere, chances are they are not the top performers you want in the first place. This is why I urge any leader to learn as much about and, if practical, participate in any training their people go through. The more information you have about what your people experience, the deeper the pool of knowledge you can draw on to make the best decisions possible for all concerned.

An interested and involved leader will breed higher-quality followers. People want and need to take pride in great leaders. And they take great pride in being part of a Team led by a dynamic and inspiring person. Be the leader who attracts the best and the brightest. They will have confidence that on your watch their ideas and concerns will be weighed and considered.

I'm proud that I worked for my last X.O. (executive officer) when I was an enlisted man. This man was in tune with the Team concept and what was going on with every one of the two-hundred-plus men under his care. When other SEALs ask me who the executive officer of my last Team was, I take special pride in telling them who and why.

It seemed that whenever anyone had a problem, he knew about it. The SEAL Team environment is chaotic in that Teammates are constantly moving and rarely in town. At any one time, three or four of the sixteen platoon members may be gone receiving advanced skills training. If a SEAL found himself in a bind while detached from his platoon, the X.O. immediately accepted and shouldered the responsibility of resolving the situation. This involved anything from procuring plane tickets for emergency leave to pay problems, and it always resulted in extended work hours. If the situation required him to stick his neck out, he wouldn't punish you if he felt you had learned your lesson; however, he would remind you the next time he saw you in the bar—the price of a pint was well worth it! I know men who have chosen their next duty station based on his presence.

A "do as I do" leader would not chastise a Team member for taking a smoke break as his very own thumb spins the knurled wheel to light the cigarette he has just put to his lips. These little things have serious ramifications on the morale and structural integrity of a Team.

I worked for an officer who was a good man and an able leader. On occasion, however, he would ask his platoon, "Are you guys gonna get any work done today?" as he stood there with a burrito or doughnut in one hand and a coffee cup from the local trend-setting coffee joint in the other. Most of the time it was in jest, but when his men were cold, tired, and hungry, they missed the humor. We knew he was a good guy, but our perception at that time was the reality.

The best SEAL officers I've worked with lead from the field, not the sidelines. When there is a difficult task that would benefit from their personal experience, they postpone their other tasks, roll up their sleeves, and *teach* their men. That time spent with their men often results in many after-hours sessions for these officers, since they must then finish their own work. Even so, they gain better-trained and increasingly loyal men.

If you never take the time to be among your workforce, you will never move beyond the typical us-versus-them scenario. This management environment is designed to let those in charge maintain a touch of anonymity and mystery, which bolsters their ability to control. As a leader, you do not want to control people; you want to convince them. If you are only in control, you have not achieved true success. You push a button and you get the expected result.

Great and prolific leaders provide their people with the internal motivation to want to complete the assigned task. When you achieve this as a Team leader, you will experience exponential success. You have a choice: Do you want your people to provide mindless programmed responses or internally motivated collaborative results?

At times, you may think that your team possesses the qualities of cooperation, camaraderie, and cohesiveness and yet you are not getting such extraordinary results. Examine your situation more closely. If you have camaraderie, is it segregated between workers and managers or divided into cliques? In either case, there is your problem. The spirit of each member working for the good of the others must encompass the entire Team.

During my time in Naval Special Warfare I have had the honor and privilege of working with the most intensely professional men I have ever known. This is not to say that they were inhuman and devoid of personality—quite the contrary. Some of the traits and qualities I consider to be the most important to leadership are flexibility, stamina, reliability, and perspective.

Even so, the three most important words in leadership are *consistency, consistency,* and *consistency.* Whether you are the best leader or the worst, happy or morose, friendly or introverted, if you are consistently that, then your people know what to expect and can work with it. A boss whose persona vacillates like the imagination of a child makes for an unsettling—and ultimately ineffective and divisive—work environment. As a leader, you will have to change; you just can't change drastically and every ten minutes.

*Flexibility,* which we will explore in greater detail later, provides you with the ability to handle unexpected situations. It is important to have a plan for possible problems, but the ability to step outside the box when something unexpected crops up is a powerful leadership tool.

When we speak of *stamina* as a leadership attribute, it does not mean that you need to be able to jump on the treadmill for an hour and then march another five or six miles. When there is a crisis or a leadership challenge, you must be able to see it through. If a particular situation needs your attention, your Team must know that you will stick with it until it is fixed. If you do have a person who is not operating in the Team's best interest, you must be able to stay strong and collected while handling the issue. If you are mentally weak and break down under stress, your Team will lose faith and confidence in you. This is the beginning of a rapid end.

*Reliability* is different from consistency. If you say that working this Saturday means that everyone gets next Friday off, you had better deliver. When you say that failure to be punctual carries a prescribed penalty, you must follow through. You will find that when your reliability is on the line, your leadership stamina will be in play as well. Tough, extraordinary times will truly test your mettle and will provide the moments when you will be most closely observed by your Team. Your Team members will be keen to evaluate you and will want to know that their leader is the best and most able. So you must be on your game at all times when you lead a Team.

*Perspective* is where your intuition and experience will be your greatest asset. If a situation does get out of hand and requires you to remove yourself to get a better look, keep your perspective. The ardent maintenance of perspective will prevent knee-jerk reactions that can be powerfully damaging.

My first platoon OIC was among the most dynamic leaders I have worked with. His personality, leadership, and teachings left a lasting impression on me. He was a friend, but during working hours there was no doubt that he was in charge. What he expected from us in cooperation and performance was always crystal clear. We also never wondered who would take care of us.

Military life is very fluid. When you are at a command, people -transfer in and out regularly. SEAL Team sailors form the tightest bonds with their fellow platoon members because they are with those men the most. Although years may pass when old Frogmen don't see each other, all that distance evaporates once they are reunited.

In the Navy, depending upon which warfare community you belong to, you can find out where old teammates are working. You can get their telephone numbers and e-mail addresses from a database. When I was working on my application package for a commissioning program, I received an e-mail message from my first OIC. About ten minutes later the phone rang, and he was on the line.

It had been at least three years since I had spoken to him. We told a few quick "sea stories" and caught up. We had both been promoted since we'd last met, and the congratulations were plentiful. I began to explain that I was after a commission. Before I'd finished my sentence, he'd offered to write a letter of recommendation.

Then I learned something simple but crucial to leadership. I said that I missed our old platoon and that I'd enjoyed working for him. There was a brief silence. Then he said, with some authority, "No, no, no . . . you didn't work for me. You worked with me. We worked together!"

I realize that this idea doesn't seem very profound, but it made a huge impact on my leadership tactics. It was as if I had insulted him by saying that I had worked *for* him. He was the epitome of a Team leader. Unfortunately, shortly after he wrote the letter for me, he was killed. I'd known that in this line of work I would lose friends. But my pal had not only been a good friend; he'd also been a mentor. His death was particularly hard for me because he was the first Teammate I'd lost—and, to this day, perhaps the closest. He was that kind of leader, and I will always take pride in the fact that I was one of his men.

Another defining point in my development as a leader occurred on my last assignment before leaving the enlisted ranks. I was deployed with my platoon, and the executive officer of the unit to which we were attached was a seasoned veteran with an unparalleled reputation. He had started in the Navy as an E-1, the lowest rank, and worked his way up to lieutenant commander.

One of the men in my platoon had slammed the back door of our Navy van, shattering the window, so we decided to turn the van in to the motor pool for replacement. The standing rule was that the vehicles were to be kept orderly at all times. It was the rainy season, though, and in our haste to get the van repaired, we turned it in without cleaning out our trash from the previous evening. Meanwhile, the X.O., whose many duties included the fiscal health of the unit, decided he wanted to see the damage he was about to pay for.

He was less than thrilled with the state of the vehicle and had a talk with our chief. The chief proceeded to read us the riot act for making the platoon look irresponsible and threatened to take away the use of all the vehicles if we couldn't care for them. We knew we should have cleaned it, but we were at a loss to understand the intensity of his anger.

A short while later the X.O. came to speak with the entire platoon. He sat down and quite calmly stated, "Hey, guys. I am pretty disappointed in how you treated that van. I know accidents happen, but I work hard to get you guys the best transportation I can, and I would hope you would not make me look foolish when I am the one who said you guys deserved to have better vehicles." You should have seen the faces in the room after that simple little speech. A roomful of hardened SEALs hung their heads, embarrassed at having disappointed their X.O.

He didn't jump up and down, because he didn't need to. He had set the stage. He was consistent, reliable, and flexible; he could go forever both physically and mentally; and he never forgot where he'd come from. The executive officer always had our best interests in mind, and we all knew it. And now we knew that we had let him down. A broken van window and a few fast-food wrappers do not count as a life-and-death matter, but the way the X.O. handled the situation was a valuable lesson in leadership. A few calm words from a dynamic, skilled leader who had set the stage for professionalism was all it took to fix the problem and to prevent future occurrences.

On rare occasions a leader can bend the rules and still be great. Before I was picked up for my commission I worked in the training cell. The training officer was an intense and unique man. He had started as an enlisted man and at the time held the rank of lieutenant junior grade. He bent the rules because he was a bit arrogant and had a tendency to always be right and know the best way to do the job. He also had a great deal of experience and knowledge. On the rare occasions when he did screw up, all eyes were upon him and everyone was quick to judge. We knew how he was, and his personality was such that he would bounce right back. What made him great was that if you were one of his men and needed help, he turned that same intensity, arrogance, and zeal into unwavering support. He may have been perceived as self-righteous and aloof by those who didn't know him, but his attitude was always geared toward Team success.

# Chapter 5 Lessons

➤ Exemplify the Team spirit. Lead from the field, not the sidelines. Be like the quarterback, not the coach!

➤ Take the time to invest in your Team, not your leisure. If you make sure that your Team is trained and motivated, you will be able to concentrate on your work and, in turn, will have time to enjoy on your own while they complete their tasks.

➤ Reinforce the idea that your Team is working with you, not for you.

➤ Consistency, consistency, consistency.

➤ Flexibility: Be able to change dynamically when given unique circumstances.

➤ Stamina: Outlast the issues you face. If you fail to do so, you will fail your Team. When you fail your Team, it will fail.

➤ Reliability: Be what you say you are going to be and do what you say you are going to do.

➤ Perspective: Keep it!

# CHAPTER 6
## *Handling Burnout*

Every Team is going to have a different mission and a different barometer for success. It follows that your Team members' tolerances for the everyday work of the mission are going to vary from those of other Teams. Factors such as maturity, prior training, personal thresholds, experiences, and personality will be major contributors to each member's drive, initiative, and stamina, for both the physical and the mental aspects of your mission. Anyone stuck in the same routine will wear out eventually. As a Team leader, you need to be able to see the warning signs of burnout and make changes to keep your people interested, energized, and motivated.

The best way to train yourself to notice the characteristics of burnout is to become a "people watcher," both in and outside of the workplace. Observe and analyze how people interact with one another. Look at different types of body language and how they affect the relationship of the people involved. Be aware that men and women express themselves physically quite differently. This is neither positive, negative, nor even something we need to change. However, it is a facet of human relations we should understand and, in fact, must understand if we want to be effective and productive leaders.

The greatest leaders strive to understand how and why people do things. Knowing these things, they are better able to effect change and glean the most from their Team members. As a leader, you should not coddle your people or wipe their noses after every sniffle. Rather, you should understand why things happen and then determine the best course of action to improve a situation. Avoiding burnout is all about reading your people, analyzing what is going on, viewing as many aspects of an issue as possible, and understanding different possible perceptions. I challenge you to learn and cultivate a greater understanding of human relations. You will become a better leader.

The Navy SEAL Team is a unique model of human behavior. The Teams consist of the most honorable, dedicated, stoic, competitive, yet *Team oriented* men anywhere. Every action, goal, and training exercise is a competition and is about beating the other guy—but *never* to his detriment or that of the Team. Every competitive scenario is geared toward pushing your Teammates to better themselves and to improve the overall quality and effectiveness of the Team.

The manner in which we deal with one another may not be appropriate for all Teams, but the principle upon which our conduct is based does apply. We push one another to excel. We are ardent defenders of morale. The concept of never leaving a man behind transcends every aspect of our lives. If a man is down in the field, we carry him out. If a man is not performing to his ability, we find out why and what we can do to fix the problem. Our Team is only as strong as the weakest, most inefficient, lowest-performing man.

You determine your own Team standards and expected levels of performance. Your leadership drives the Team, and the Team polices itself.

Peer pressure will drive less motivated individuals to become more productive Team members. A clear and concise mission statement sets a solid standard and makes it possible for you to determine when your people might begin to become overwhelmed.

Burnout occurs for many reasons. An individual can be overworked and exhausted, underworked and not challenged, properly worked but unappreciated. Team members can feel patronized or used. They can feel alone in the crowd or as if they don't fit in with the group, although they may interact well with other Team members. All of this causes stress, which can lead to depression, low morale, and a feeling of not caring for the mission or the Team. In the end, if you do not have solid standards for performance, your people will become worn out and it will be difficult for you to recognize when they are nearing exhaustion. Rapid identification and rectification of problems or difficult situations will serve you, your individual Team members, and the Team. Catching a problem early will make its solution easier and will send a message to your Team. The time you spend caring for their problems will illustrate to your Team members that you are genuinely interested in their well-being and that you are a hands-on leader. This alone may solve many of your problems, because many Team inefficiencies and morale problems that can lead to burnout stem from the perception that the leadership does not care about the workforce.

A person continually going that extra mile to complete tasks will suffer from overwork and exhaustion. Sometimes it will be necessary for you to increase the Team's or an individual Team member's workload near a deadline or for a special project. For the most part, people can and will accept this. But when people who give 110 percent are continually called upon for additional duties, they will burn out. Extra incentives or remuneration can help, but only to a certain extent. When you take advantage of people and their work ethic, it will become obvious to the Team—even in situations where you give that extra pay or additional time off. The word will spread through the Team, creating misunderstandings or bad feelings. And since perception is reality, until you do something to change that perception, you will be stuck with even bigger problems than meeting deadlines or completing special projects.

Regardless of the goal, and whether it's short- or long-term, you must consider the ramifications of the added stresses to your Team members' morale. Chances are that your people will hide their distaste for the continual added responsibility out of duty or loyalty, or because they want or need a good job evaluation or an increase in pay. You should keep an eye on those who do not make a fuss. In the SEALs we understand that a complaining sailor is a happy sailor. Once he stops complaining, he has stopped caring. The caveat is that your Team members must never complain for the sake of complaint, but only to effect some sort of change. Encourage your people to come to you with a quiver full of solutions for the problems they have or see. Encourage unrest, as long as it is constructive.

Often your best employees will work and work, asking for nothing in return. It can be easy to overlook these pillars of the Team and take them for granted. But a small effort on your part recognizing jobs well done will pay huge dividends. Most of these performers just want the satisfaction of a productive day or to know that their efforts are noticed. They are not glory hounds, but it is important that they be recognized. Even if they stay late on their own initiative, thank them each and every time. That is usually enough. You will find that this small action alone can sustain their motivation. If those Team members ever come to you for help, do everything you can to see that they are accommodated.

In my last platoon there was a guy we called Hollywood. Ironically, he was anything but. He was a big fellow from Hawaii, virtually bullet-proof. Hollywood was quiet and professional, and he excelled at everything he did. He was also a solid friend, boundless with humor and camaraderie. While we were on deployment, I was shocked one day to hear him fly into a tirade about something insignificant. Those of us on his Team looked at one another in confusion, then let it go and went about our business. But it happened again about a week later.

That night the platoon got together for drinks in the barracks TV lounge, which we had made into a pub. The unit X.O., the same man who had secured the vans for us, had won our right to maintain it, even though the base C.O. discouraged it. One of our guys had built a bar and some shelving, and we'd covered the walls and ceiling with camou-flage netting and other Team paraphernalia and memorabilia.

We were having a great time, but Hollywood was silent. Finally a couple of us began to poke at him. One guy said, "Hey, Hollywood . . . what's with you?" Tirade number three! He screamed about the work he had done over the past year or so, the late hours he had put in, and the fact that nobody seemed to notice. Others had been recognized, but not him. After a short silence, one of the guys said, "Thanks, Hollywood." Hollywood looked up, smiled, and said, "Now, was that so hard?" The room erupted in laughter!

That was a powerful lesson. Here was this amazingly hardworking and dedicated Team member. He didn't want an award. He didn't want a raise. He didn't want his picture in the paper. All he wanted was for somebody to say thanks.

Overusing your experienced people for the difficult tasks and neglecting to notice and develop your "new people" is a waste of valuable assets. Take the time to train your new people and give them a chance to shine. Don't destroy your best people because everything is an emergency and needs their particular attention. Set up a mentoring program and have the experienced Team members work with the new people.

If you always use the same people for the challenging jobs, you will stifle others who want to be challenged. Can you remember how you felt when the teacher always called on the same person? You stopped raising your hand. You stopped contributing, although you had better ideas and more drive to learn. The same thing will occur on your Team if you overwork a faithful few and forget your obligations to those not yet experienced. The perception of favoritism will cause resentment. You must never lose sight of the fact that it is your duty to train all your Team members, and part of that training involves developing and placing faith in the "new guys."

The more you push your newer Team members to the side and count on the experience of the seasoned people, the more the new people will lose their motivation. Give them a chance to prove what they can do. When people are involved, they feel important. They have a greater sense of pride, which fosters a more solid and productive work ethic, and one that is catching.

When people learn that your Team is a place where they can develop, grow, and use their talents, you will draw the best of the lot.

When you and your Team are dynamic and successful, people will want to be a part of it.

When I arrived at my first SEAL Team, I, like my fellow "new guys," wanted to get to work as soon as possible. My mind was bursting with new knowledge and tactics, and I was anxious to prove my worth. However, every time we had a high-profile training operation, the "head shed," or Team leader, put in the really seasoned guys. I knew I could go in there and perform, but I couldn't get the chance. How could I become an experienced old guy without experience? I became frustrated. I kept my mouth shut and my ears open, but after a short while I had had enough. I asked to meet with the chief and OIC, and I mentioned my concerns, explaining that I wanted a chance to prove myself. They said they'd been thinking only of the success of the Team and not my personal ambition. We talked for about thirty minutes before they decided that I would perform a key role in the next operation. I was stoked and popped out of my chair to go get my gear ready. As I left the room, my OIC said, "Hey, you just stuck it out there. If it gets cut off, it's on you . . . so don't make us look bad." I understood that I had challenged the decisions he had made and there would be no room for error.

The operation went off without a hitch. I was thrilled, as it was my first important training mission as a SEAL. After the debriefing, the chief approached me and said with a smile, "Thanks for not screwing up." The message was that he was proud of my performance and approved of my tenacity. It felt great to be useful.

There are also people who do what is expected of them and perform to the standards you have set. But they feel invisible. The good news is that this is also probably the easiest problem to fix. Save the fan-fare for those who exceed the standards. When, however, you have Team members who have been with you for a while, who are present and on time every day, and who do their jobs to the standards you have set, make sure you notice them. If you have a company newsletter, thank them in it, or give them an extra day off; there are any number of suit-able rewards that say, "I appreciate your efforts. You are a welcome and valuable member of the Team."

One of the worst feelings as a Team member is that your contribu-tions and efforts are for naught. When you assign someone a task, empower them sufficiently so that they can complete it. If you trust them enough to make it theirs, let it be theirs—unless, of course, they are going to get somebody hurt. Burnout from frustration is a very real threat, and recovery from it is hard.

Mentoring is a powerful tool when properly implemented and monitored. If you are going to use your hot runners to train the new people or the nonperformers, let them do so the way they see fit. People will burn out faster when they feel they can't put forth their best efforts. After all, you delegated the task to them because they are closer to the situation and have a better working knowledge of its intricacies. Don't put your best assets in a position to fail. Don't let them perceive that they are failing. Many people have personal standards unique to them and it can be very damaging if those standards are not satisfied. You cannot task someone with improving the nonperformers, then tie their hands and make them incapable of reaching their own goals, or effecting any real change or improvement. This can be as damaging, if not more so, than overworking them.

As I mentioned, before I started the ROTC program, I spent two months in Newport, Rhode Island, for an indoctrination course. I was dissatisfied with the physical fitness level of the majority of the other officer candidates. By Navy standards, the majority of the men passed, but just barely. If you are going to be in front, you need to be worthy of that position in every way. I wasn't satisfied with the intensity of the three mandatory physical fitness sessions I was required to attend per week, so I offered to run them. In addition, I volunteered my time to run the extra P.T. (physical training) sessions, required for those who had failed the physical readiness test (PRT) or were over their body-fat limits.

My superiors agreed, and I had the class for two months before the next PRT. I made a plan to run them hard but smart. I explained that I wouldn't have them do any physically damaging exercises, and I promised that if they gave me their best effort, I would improve their conditioning. A healthy body, I said, creates and supports a sharper mind. I offered after-hours time to those who wanted nutritional advice or one-on-one P.T. help.

At the beginning, many of my classmates couldn't do all I asked of them. I told them that it was better to do what they could perfectly than to do all the exercises improperly. A couple of weeks into the program a few people complained to the staff that I was being too hard on them. They said that they weren't SEALs and I shouldn't demand so much from them. I explained to the staff that the sessions I conducted weren't as rigorous as those I'd experienced as a SEAL. Furthermore, my goal was the vast improvement and development of both their bodies and their knowledge of fitness.

Still, I was ordered to reduce the intensity of the workouts. I was furious! I had spent my own off time to improve the class. Now I was being told to dial back because a few of my classmates felt I'd set the bar too high. At the next session, I was handed a script. I looked it over and asked, "This is just the warm-up, right?" I was appalled by the low standards. Many of my classmates had told me enthusiastic stories about how they hadn't felt so good in years due to the previous workouts; now I was ordered to lower the bar.

I explained to the staff that I was getting results and said that I found it sickening that the entire class should lower themselves to the level of the unmotivated and weak. Nevertheless, I was asked to stick with the script. I did not want to undermine the staff, but after two sessions of the "new" program, I'd had enough. People were unaware that I was ordered to alter the workouts and asked what was wrong and why had I made them so easy. The disappointment was obvious in the faces of the majority to the men and women who had realized for the first time in their lives that they could really push themselves. I went to the staff to get them to change their minds and put me in control again. They refused, and I offered to step down, being unwilling to support mediocrity. They asked me to stay in my position, and I did so with the hope that they would soon see my point.

Near the beginning, we had run in the snow, freezing rain, and leet. While everyone else bundled up, I ran in shorts and a T-shirt to prove that mental power was key—and besides, soaking wet sweatpants and sweatshirts get really heavy and uncomfortable. One day, we were on a 2.5-mile run in mixed rain and snow. The frigid wind off the sound cut right through our wet clothes. I could not stand the political bickering about the workouts anymore, so I ran among the men about chanting, *"If it doesn't suck, we don't do it!"* That, coupled with an occasional overenthusiastic, *"Yeah yeah yeaahhhh,"* started to fend off the cold. Soon the class was echoing these utterances. This kind of motivation is contagious, and by the end everyone was joking and "reminiscing" about the toils of the run they had completed just some five minutes prior. Attitudes were changing. Once we were back in the gym, I told the class that something easy never makes a good story.

Soon, the majority of the class started to jeer me for making the PTs too easy. The spirit of Team competition had taken over. The class began to demand more from one another and from me.

You want this to happen. You want the Team to delegate the task of moral management to themselves. The class I led now had internalized a much higher standard, and it was blatantly obvious in their performance. I cranked up the P.T.s to even higher levels than before. And the class loved it! The gym filled with motivated taunts and yells for more pain. For the next few weeks we trained like animals, and the staff never said a word. When the class took the final PRT, the numbers of push-ups and sit-ups had skyrocketed. Run times had dropped by minutes for each person. Only one person had never joined the Team. He'd remained a lone individual and stayed out of shape. He had never come to me for help or advice. In fact, I'd told him halfway through that I did not feel he belonged, that his heart wasn't in it. He said they wouldn't kick him out after he'd made it this far. Indeed, the staff had considered waiving his requirements so that he could graduate from the program. But the rest of the class was outraged. They had all worked their butts off and earned their scores—now they were seeing that it didn't matter.

I approached the staff and conveyed the sentiments of the Team. The failing man was dropped from the program the next day.

If your people begin to reach burnout when completing normal duties, look for other problems: illness, troubles at home, not being suited for the job. If the entire Team approaches burnout, are your standards too high? An engine is designed to propel a car, but if you stress it, it will break.

Rewards can be a very powerful tool; use them as such if necessary. Rewards are important. Your rewards will be unique to your situation and resources. If you can give a raise or bonus, do so. If you can give some sort of meaningful award, do so. Whatever you do, it must be sincere. Empty thanks and token awards do more damage than good. Find out what people want, and remember that not everyone will respond the same way to every reward. Be original; think of something new.

Set your standards high and let the Team do the work. When your Team sets high standards for itself and expects that level of performance from all of its members, don't deflate their morale and motivation by coddling the nonperformers and the weak. What message do you want to send your people? When you expect the best from them and most of them deliver, don't accept anything less than that from the others. If your people see you accepting less than mediocre effort from an individual, you will lose credibility and power. Watch your Team and be flexible enough to adapt and develop with them.

# Chapter 6 Lessons

➢ Be a student of human interaction.

➢ Do not take advantage of your Team!

➢ Burnout will engender low morale.

➢ Be mindful of your Team's morale level.

➢ Identify and quench burnout before it happens.

➢ Motivate your Team to be the custodian of its own morale.

➢ Know your people and their personal standards; deviation from those standards may indicate a looming or manifested problem.

➢ False or petty rewards can often do more damage than good.

# CHAPTER 7
## *Flexibly Inflexible*

When I arrived in southern California to attend BUD/S, I was in great physical condition. I had been running, swimming, and lifting almost every day of the week. My very first physical evolution at BUD/S was a four-mile soft-sand conditioning run. I had been training in soft sand and felt that I was well prepared for the task. By the second mile of this instructor-led run, however, I was sucking wind like never before and attracting the concern of a couple of the instructors.

After a few weeks of this, my class proctor, the instructor in charge of the class, approached me. He explained that he could tell I was giving 110 percent, but that I was unable to stay with the front of the pack because I was running *wrong*. I gave him a puzzled look. I had played sports my entire life and thought that I was a good runner. He took the time to show me how to run properly, which was very uncomfortable at first. My entire life I had run with my arms pumping vigorously by my sides. He explained that all this did was tighten up my chest, restricting both its expansion and my oxygen-uptake efficiency. The revised technique was to let my arms relax by my sides with very little back and forth movement. If you run like I used to, try this new arm style. It took me several weeks to adapt and accept this change, but it made all the difference in the world. The lesson I learned is that what seems comfortable now may not always be the best or most effective way.

Flexibility is one of the major qualities required to cross over from the old managerial paradigm to the dynamic, fulfilling, and challenging environment of a Team leader. Nothing is absolute, and you must be ready to adjust when the need arises. It is when you leave the confines of archaic and restrictive thinking that you begin to recognize hidden potential in both your subordinates and yourself. You must develop a sense for what is and is not an acceptable level of deviation from the expected tier of performance.

Inflexibility is tantamount to stagnation, which is not conducive to progress. The ability to adapt and bring your Team with you is one of the traits of a great leader. Although I advocate flexibility, this in no way means that you should ever compromise your standards; that is where it pays to remain inflexible.

Do not fear change. For some, this will be hard to accept, because it requires departure from the traditional model of management, where ideas about people, their duties, and the roles of the leader are fixed. In military school and boot camp I was taught to do what I was told, when I was told, and nothing else but what I was told, no questions asked. This is all well and good if you have a huge force of people to move, control, or direct to lead in the completion of a task. But if you treat your handpicked professional Team members like mindless sheep, you will soon find yourself left with just that: a bunch of disgruntled, moderately productive sheep. You will not reap the benefits of a satiated and fulfilled staff. Overmanipulation and control leads to micromanagement, a debilitating menace. You should not be flexing your authority and coercing others to do your bidding. You should be working with them for the benefit of each individual and for the good of the Team itself. To be effective in a dynamic situation, you must be ready and willing to deviate from your comfortable norm when that's what's required to successfully complete the task.

If your Team consists of twelve people, you will have the advantage of twelve perspectives and twelve different views. Capitalize on this diversity. If you remain aloof and unapproachable, you will remain alone and unapproached. The entire purpose of leadership is to effect change through the organized efforts and collaboration of the whole, rather than the direction of one, as in the typical management paradigm.

The size of your organization will dictate the amount and quality of the contact you have with your Team. This is where you must consider the ramifications of an effective chain of command. Be who you want your subordinates to be. The way you treat your Team of leaders will affect how those people treat their workers. When you set the example of being flexible and willing to adapt, your attitude will filter through the organization. Reap your rewards by making it known that the entire Team is welcome and expected to proffer new ideas and suggestions. At the same time, institute a policy of "No complaints without solutions." This will help eliminate frivolous griping and will force your personnel to think critically and creatively to solve problems on their own. Ultimately, your employees and Team members will become more involved and conscientious.

You cannot plan for every scenario ahead of time. What you must do when approaching a situation is review lessons learned from previous events and situations, formulate a collaborative plan for action based on the Team's goals, and put the plan up for scrutiny. Then, time permitting, tear it apart, look for holes, and plug them with contingency plans.

Few of us enjoy an abundance of time. We must maximize every second. The beauty of reviewing lessons learned is that they allow you to narrow the focus and scope of the what-ifs. What went wrong last time, and why? How was the situation resolved before? Was that the best way to fix it, or can we do better if it happens again? You need to ask these questions before, during, and after any situation.

Be wary of complacency because it ruins morale; it will end up hurting Team members and the Team itself. In the SEALs, complacency can kill, literally, and I know men who have died of this Team (or sometimes individual) ailment. On the professional level, complacency can allow the Team to become inefficient, let it be consumed by internal and external competition, and subject Team members to burnout—another fatal Team disease.

It is imperative to have a well-thought-through and -practiced plan for action. Open your mind and remain one step ahead of potential problems. When encountering a problem, you must be willing to reassess the situation and decide whether to continue as planned or take a new course of action.

I have been in situations that have ended undesirably when seasoned veterans were unwilling to accept new ideas. They argued, "This is how we did it in my last three platoons." But what worked well then didn't work this time. In situations like this, evaluate what happened and record lessons learned for next time. Rely on the experience of your seasoned Team members. But remember that just because someone is new or junior does not mean that they cannot have a great idea or solution to a problem. Pull from as *many* resources as time allows; consider your options, then act.

Do not asphyxiate your Team by closing them out in times of crisis. There will be cases when there is not enough time, nor is it a good idea, to consult everyone and consider their thoughts. But when you do have the time, take it! Allow your Team to be part of the solution. It is dangerous and foolish to close them out. When your people stop coming up with ideas or different ways to do things, that is when you need to be concerned. You have either shut them out or killed their morale. Keep innovation alive.

In addition to contingencies, SEALs always develop a set of "Go" and "No go" criteria before embarking on any operation. The final call is always made on the scene, and, to minimize the errors of judgment inherent to crisis situations, is based on a solid set of criteria established beforehand. Predetermined criteria are an aid to assist the Team, but we must still be able to analyze and adapt on the spot. We look at what it will take to complete a mission, the importance of the mission, and the minimum assets required. What if certain equipment is damaged during insertion—will that compromise the ability to complete the mission? What is the maximum number of casualties or injured the Team can sustain before the operation is no longer feasible? Is there a certain time after which it will be too late to get the job done?

If it is at all possible to rehearse a plan, speech, presentation, or procedure, rehearse it. In the SEALs we will plan a mission similar to what we have done many times before, but we will always rehearse the current plan. Repetition breeds familiarity, and once you know a situation, you can analyze it better. Flexibility plays a major role in this process as well. If you are on your last practice run and you find a flaw, you must have the discipline to stop, analyze the plan, and change it if necessary. The rehearsal process must start over, but when the operation goes off without a hitch, it is well worth the time. The first time you execute your plan should not be during the actual situation. It is imperative to factor in time for rehearsals and review. Make the mistakes in the comfort of your Team area, where the situation can be controlled and modified, not in the field, where it may be too late.

Another facet of flexibility is the willingness to allow your people to make mistakes. Nobody is perfect, not any of us. The mistakes we make, and how we handle and learn from them, define who we are. Do you wallow in a quagmire of self-pity and remorse, or do you analyze what went wrong, reformulate your plan of attack, and reassert yourself?

If you maintain a log of lessons learned and use mentoring to ensure effective information dispersal among your Team members, you will be less likely to encounter problems. If your people are making mistakes, however, it means they are trying. If they make more mistakes later, it means they have enough drive and personal motivation to brush themselves off and try again. That is perseverance, and that is what you want.

If no one on your Team makes mistakes, you are either the luckiest leader in the world or your people are so afraid of collapse (or of you) that they are unwilling to risk failing and the ensuing harsh consequences. You want dreamers and risk takers who are striving to improve, who are willing to make mistakes along they way, learn from them, and continue on. This process, of course, must withstand the test of reasonableness. If an individual is making the same error time and again, you have other issues to deal with. But when a person is intent on success,

71

it is both possible and probable that they will fall on their face a few times. Record the lessons learned, reevaluate, and reattack.

All too often people are unwilling to let others develop. At the first sign of trouble or the first stumble, they don their cape and race to the rescue. Unless it is a life-threatening situation, all this does is frustrate and demoralize the individual and, ultimately, the Team. How will it be possible for your subordinates to realize the consequences of their mistakes, personal and professional, if the overcontrolling manager intervenes every time any difficulty arises? Team members must be held accountable for their actions, but at the same time provisions should be made to accommodate the learning process.

There will be times when you have to discipline your Team members. That, too, is a part of leadership. If disciplinary action is to be taken for a mistake, let it also be known that extra efforts are noticed and appreciated. When Team members understand that they are allowed to make mistakes if they do so with honorable intentions but will be held accountable nonetheless, they will focus their efforts. They will still take risks in the interest of advancement but with greater reverence and care.

From day one of BUD/S training to your operational SEAL platoon, the instructors drill into your head that you must train the way you fight. It is always real, since 90 percent of the training we conduct uses live bullets and explosives. There is always a chance that someone may get killed.

When I was on my first SEAL Team, I had the opportunity to attend the Naval Special Warfare scout sniper course. I had graduated BUD/S almost two years prior and had been working like crazy ever since. I had learned to take every training exercise seriously and treat it as if it were the real thing. One day in sniper school, I was on a patrolling and reconnaissance exercise. I had done what seemed to be two hundred of these missions already, and I was tired. At dusk, I was approaching the suspected target area. In the SEALs, we recognize a prescribed distance around a target as a hostile area. I was well within this domain for this operation.

In these situations, SEALs are supposed to be extra sensitive to their surroundings, taking in every chirp of a bird or rustle of a leaf. We walk slowly, allowing our senses to adapt to the environment, analyzing light and abnormal tree shapes. We calculate every step for pressure, noise, and print left behind. Scents carried on the wind can make your spine tingle, like when you smell the smoldering fire at the target sight. Your rifle is a split second from its place at your shoulder, your thumb ready to deactivate the safety, your trigger finger poised on the trigger guard, ready to slip into place. Your eyes are wide and your mouth slightly open, to receive that extra bit of sound. Eliminating one sense heightens the others. Every couple of meters you stop to scan; then you close your eyes momentarily to heighten your listening senses.

There I was, within five hundred meters of the target, my stance erect and my rifle by my side in my right hand . . . not ready to go at all! I had relaxed my posture because of fatigue, and at that moment I learned that in the game of war, the second you let your guard down, your enemy will kill you. I took two more steps and looked up. Twenty meters ahead of me, standing in the middle of the trail, was one of my instructors, arms folded across his chest, head shaking in disappointment. I had not seen him. This was not because he was hidden at all; in fact, he was standing in the open. The low light coupled with my lack of attention allowed me to get that close before noticing him. I looked at him for a second or two, gathered myself, and got back into the scenario, adopting the techniques of stealth taught by the instructors. I immediately stepped into my heightened senses, melted into the forest, and continued on my way as if the incident had not taken place. This was not the time to reflect on my mistake; it was the time to concern myself wholly with the job at hand and to complete it to the utmost of my ability. There would be time to lament later.

After every operation, training or real, we have a comprehensive debriefing to identify both good and bad points. This is a time when all is laid out and nothing is personal. Everything that comes up is mentioned strictly to improve the Team and to prevent such a mistake again. The instructor who saw me never mentioned it to anyone, and we have never discussed it. He made a judgment call. He chose not to bring up my indiscretion to the class. Had it not been for my track record, I believe I would have been kicked out of the school, but this man stepped outside of the box and realized that his piercing gaze of disappointment was all the reprimand I needed. Another instructor might have seen only right and wrong and made the situation public, but this one did not. I had made a mistake, and we both knew it. In a real-world scenario, this same mistake could get me or my Teammates killed. In that brief moment of unspoken counseling, I decided—and he knew—that I would never let my professionalism wane again. Until now there were only two individuals that knew of this event, which has haunted me every day since it occurred.

Successful leaders do not fit into one mold. Leadership, by its very nature, is an entity of change and diversity. The great difference between a leader and a manager is that the leader has the courage and takes the latitude to stray from the norm, develop a vision, share it with the Team, and go after that vision together with the Team. As a leader, you will be required to handle everything from strictly business situations to the intricacies of the personal lives of your Team members. You must be ready and able to approach these issues with the guidance, assistance, and support of your Team.

If you are a staunch subscriber to the outdated management model of achieving common goals, you may survive but will lose untold wealth, both monetary and human. You must be involved with the Team and concern yourself with the Team's concerns. If you are cognizant and flexible, you will avoid desperation and knee-jerk reactions. When you function as a Team, collaborate, rehearse, and attend to lessons learned, you will enjoy greater success.

## Chapter 7 Lessons

➤ Allow people to make mistakes; that is how we learn.

➤ The way a person handles and learns from a mistake helps define them.

➤ Before taking action against someone who has made a mistake, carefully consider whether it was done with malice aforethought, was carelessness, or was simply an honest mistake.

➤ If you rush in to remedy a mistake before it comes to fruition, your people will become complacent and rely on you to fix everything.

➤ Let your Team members learn and develop.

➤ Avoid knee-jerk reactions.

➤ Practice accountability and encouragement. Hold people accountable for their actions, yet do not be so overbearing as to stifle their future efforts.

➤ Remain dynamic and aggressive with regards to change and flexibility, but never at the expense of the Team, its goals, or its high standards.

# CHAPTER 8
## *The Menace of Micromanagement*

I f you know everything, you just might get the opportunity to prove it! A leader knows when to let the Team function and when to lead. You are part of a Team, and letting go and letting the Team function on its own may be one of the most difficult balancing acts you will ever perform. If you give a competent individual or group a task and empower them to accomplish it, you must accept the results, unless they adversely affect your goal.

The only good thing about micromanagement is that it can be fixed. Be wary of the impulse to micromanage and be sure to accept new ways of doing things if the results will accomplish the common goal— even if they aren't what you initially had in mind. Do not make your Team revisit work because they didn't do it the way you had learned to do it. Have faith in their experience and own creative thinking.

When you delegate and entrust projects to your Team, you will benefit from different perspectives on dealing with situations and on reaching goals, and you will gain insight into the individuals who make up your Team. If you continually second-guess and change the work of your subordinates, not only will you kill their morale and motivation, but you will create extra work for yourself. Successful leaders let their people do their jobs and concentrate on their own work. This is more than effective time management; it is an inspiring use of resources.

Organize your Team for success. When you are preparing to delegate a task, take the time to consider your options. Make sure that you choose the right person or people for the job and that you are not setting them up for failure. You will have to know whom you've got, what their talents are, and what their current workload is. Once you have this information, explain the key points or details of the tasks at hand and the objectives, or goals, of the work. Do not assume that your Team members know these from the outset. If the project is important enough to be done to exacting specifications, take the time to explain these details. Clarification of particulars in advance is professional guidance. Chastising innovation, which happens in the absence of professional guidance, is professional suicide.

If you have fully explained the parameters of a given task and the result is not what you had intended, you must find out whether it was a misunderstanding, bad intent, or a lack of attention that caused the inconsistencies. At this point you have two options. You can explain the pertinent details again, point out the flaws, and let your Team try again; or you can take the time to mentor your Team and show them what you expect. Either way, you must analyze the situation carefully before chastising them. Did you do your part and give them the information they needed? You lose credibility if you expect your Team members to be mind readers, then reprimand them when it turns out they don't have that skill.

One of the most damaging types of micromanager is the control freak. This is the person who feels compelled to control every situation.

People with this flaw force their opinions on others, even when they are not experts in the subject at hand. You must be able to recognize this tendency in yourself or your subordinates. Once you recognize it, you must fix it. Many micromanagers lack confidence and feel that they must be the center of attention and the keeper of knowledge to maintain respect. Some of these people lack the ability to trust others or simply do not want to share the glory of a job well done. Just because you are in charge does not mean that everyone is going to expect you to know everything. That is what the expertise of the Team and the individual Team members is for. You must have a working knowledge of the operations. But it is not possible for you to maintain intimate knowledge of every task required for carrying those operations out.

If you are reluctant to trust or let go, you must learn. Think of the added time you will have to complete those tasks that are truly yours.

Some micromanagers like to interfere with their subordinates for personal gain. This sort of person knows the power of information and tries to maintain a monopoly on it. They hold back key knowledge, keeping it to themselves, and only produce it when it will benefit them. This behavior is a sure morale killer.

As a competent leader, you must always think of the Team first. Everyone looks great when the Team succeeds! If the whole Team is not successful, no one is successful. If you are willing to shine and leave your Team behind, you do not belong in power.

The key to Navy SEAL success is that SEALs never leave a Teammate behind. *Never!* On your Team, every Team member must be included in the Team's success. As a Team leader, it is your responsibility to motivate those who aren't top performers. If you or any of your Team members are thinking only of themselves, you will lose the morale of the entire Team.

In all my time as a SEAL I have seen only one person who was truly a terrible leader. Everybody has his or her moments, but for this person it was a lifestyle.

One night in the southern California desert, I was the point man leading my platoon on a training mission. The point man usually carries the lightest load because he is supposed to scout ahead to determine the ideal path and spot any booby traps. The patrol order was as follows: point man, officer in charge (OIC), radioman, M-60 gunner, medic, M-60 gunner, leading petty officer (LPO), and rear security man. As the point man, my sole purpose was to select and navigate the safest route into and out of the target area. In addition, it was my responsibility to ensure that the men rested and the Team's pace accommodated the heavily laden M-60 gunners. To do this, I needed to find suitable resting spots during my probes forward. The "Pig Gunners" and Comm Guys carry quite a substantial load and require periodic breaks to stay fresh.

According to the scenario parameters for this particular exercise, global positioning system (GPS) units were considered inoperative because the enemy had knocked out the GPS satellites. But I rarely used the GPS units anyway, as I always relied on my map, compass, pace count, and terrain features. With these tools I could determine how far it was to important landmarks and reset points. In addition, I kept navigation information in my head; we were always instructed not to write it down, in case we dropped it or were captured. Another drawback to GPS units is that they store route information and could provide damaging intelligence if they were to fall into enemy hands.

It was standard operating procedure (SOP) for our platoon that the point man be the forward eyes and ears. You can't just plop sixteen men down in hostile territory. You need to find an area that will conceal them and provide cover and defensive positions.

I took pride in being able to balance these duties. Those heavily burdened needed breaks, and I found a spot every few hundred meters. Of course, this was great for me as well, since I could separate myself and listen without the noise of the men.

I was not particularly fond of the OIC, but I'd left my personal feelings back in the barracks. I liked and needed the space in front to analyze the terrain and make good decisions. On this night, however, my OIC was never more than four feet behind me. I asked him several times to stand off, because all I could hear was the crunch of his boots against the rocks. But a minute later he would be on my heels again. Then he started asking me where my GPS was and if I knew where I was. I responded that GPS units "didn't work" here and that I knew exactly where I was.

Frustration started to set in. I was thinking, "He picked me for the job because he knew I could do it well; now he's riding my ass and hindering my work." During our next break he asked me where we were. I pulled out my poncho and covered our heads and the map. I produced a subdued red-lens flashlight and pointed out on the map where we were. Then he asked for an eight-digit grid coordinate.

While I was checking the grid, he was fiddling with his GPS. I looked at him and said, "Sir, GPSs don't work, remember?" He just looked at me and asked for the grid again. I gave him a quick grid from the large-scale map. We were in the middle of the desert in featureless terrain. I was recording our position by pace and bearing, and we were already several thousand meters into our trek. I knew where we were and where we needed to go. Then he asked if I wanted to know where we really were. I was fifteen meters off according to his GPS, which was tracking only two satellites at the time and was inaccurate.

We continued, and I did everything I could to ease my frustration. Then he started telling me where to stop for breaks. I explained that there was a wash ahead big enough to house the entire platoon, but he wanted to stop where we were, and we did—in the open, with the entire Team exposed. I crawled around to each guy to make sure my pace was good for all. A few of the guys looked at me in disbelief and asked why I had left them so exposed for our break. I explained briefly, and they understood.

We started patrolling again and, twenty meters later, we came upon the huge wash I had seen. I dealt with the OIC's micromanaging, knowing the chief would straighten the situation all out when we returned. There were several times, however, when I wanted to invite him to lead the patrol. It would have been great to see him fail. He couldn't have known the navigation plan as I did, because I was the one who'd planned it.

By the end of the night it had become blatantly obvious that the OIC had been hindering our mission. But once we recognized that the OIC was a micromanager, we were able to band together to maintain stability. For the rest of the workup and deployment, the whole of the Team stayed strong and ensured the success of the platoon. Because the rest of the Team and I were able to put Team success above the frustration the OIC caused, we were able to get into the target safely and back to our extract point without incident.

At times it may be necessary for a leader to ensure that all things are in order before an evolution. Even seasoned pilots use a checklist each and every time they fly, because they're human and can't always remember every detail of every task. Once again, the lesson-learned list becomes essential. Call it a checklist if you like, but whatever it is, it is a technique to ensure success. There is no shame in referring to it, but there is much to be lost when you fail because you didn't use the resources you had to prevent problems.

There will be times when you, or someone you appoint, must ensure success by microassessing. While preparing for a job, make it known that you expect your Team to review lessons learned and to rehearse if possible. All Team members need to realize that if they follow these simple practices, they will make fewer mistakes. Only in knowing, as completely as possible, the ways in which the Team has been successful before, how they have failed or created problems, and what their strengths and weaknesses are can you ensure the greatest possibility for success.

Navy SEALs operate at night most of the time. The veil of darkness is our friend, and we exploit it. This carries with it risks and heightens the stakes considerably. On the one hand, darkness can conceal you. On the other hand, you must negotiate unfamiliar terrain in that same obscurity. Night-vision devices are not always an option. They can ruin your natural night vision, which may become crucial. If there is not enough ambient light, such devices can be nearly useless anyway. The use of an infrared light to illuminate your target will make you a beacon to anyone else using night-vision devices.

Each member of a platoon carries an infrared strobe light and chemical sticks—break-and-shake lights like the ones kids use during

Halloween, except that these are infrared. We carry other gear that can emit some useful light. There is always the flashlight in the backpack. I carry a small penlight on a lanyard around my neck, stuffed inside my shirt. This can be turned on and concealed well enough not to be obvious to others. But when seen through night-vision goggles (NVGs), these lights, small as they are, are like beacons.

Before every night evolution, and periodically throughout it, the leading petty officer or chief will look at each member of the platoon with NVGs to ensure that all lights are secured. This is not micromanagement; this is ensuring safety and success.

There may have been times when you were sure micromanagement was necessary. Maybe the Team or person assigned a task just wasn't getting it, or perhaps there was someone who needed to be under scrutiny most of the time. Most likely, you were wrong. Micromanagement is dangerous and never appropriate. There is never a necessity for micromanagement. If at times you need to spend extra time with your people, you must remember to mentor and develop, not micromanage. People will need help and additional attention, some times more than others. But you must use these as opportunities for productive development. Learn to be a mentor rather than resorting to micromanagement.

Some people will argue that some micromanagers are innocent, that they are just doing their jobs. This situation occurs when a leader has good intentions and wants to share their knowledge but gets too involved. It is a great and powerful tool to be known among your Team as a participant, a working leader, but not at the expense of preventing your people from performing their duties. There can be a fine line between what your Team perceives as enthusiastic interest and overwhelming meddling. Your subordinates want to know that you care and are not aloof and beyond reproach, but at the same time they need their own realm in which to perform their duties.

## Chapter 8 Lessons

➤ Assign the job only if you trust the assignee to do it.

➤ Provide the necessary requirements.

➤ Do not hang over your workers' shoulders unless absolutely necessary.

➤ Do not nitpick a job well done just because it isn't a carbon copy of what you had in your mind's eye.

➤ Accept the results unless they are severely flawed or could cause an accident.

➤ Allow your Team to make and learn from mistakes, which is crucial to development.

➤ No matter how intuitive your Team members are, they are not mind readers. Give them the essential details, then trust their judgment and results.

➤ Perpetuating a trend of second-guessing work breeds resentment. Trial and error and senior guidance is advantageous; however, do not waste time by setting someone to a task ill informed.

➤ *Empowerment* is the most important principle. You hired these people to do a job . . . *let them do it!*

➤ If you "know it all," you just might get the chance to prove it!

➤ Work toward the goal. Be seen, not heard. Set the stage and let the Team go, making small steerage adjustments when necessary.

➤ Just because someone makes a mistake does not mean they require micromanagement. Consider whether they really had all the tools they needed to complete the job.

# CHAPTER 9
## *Preventive Maintenance*
## Time is money, but support is the mint!

The value of maintaining your equipment should be obvious. But it is surprising how few people recognize this and work to save themselves time, money, and heartache. Every piece of equipment you use in your business has two life expectancies—one when it is maintained and another when it is not. Just because a problem or issue has not yet manifested itself doesn't mean it is not poised to wreak havoc on your Team.

A Navy SEAL Team operates almost exclusively in harsh environments and under extreme conditions. What SEALs perceive as ideal weather keeps everyone else indoors, and we like it that way. With these great conditions comes an adverse and damaging effect on our equipment, gear, and weapons. When SEALs go into the field, all we have is what we bring with us—we only carry what we need—and it is crucial that everything work once we arrive at our objective.

Most SEAL missions originate from the water, and mostly from salt water. Salt water will corrode and damage most of our gear. It is imperative that we get it across the beach dry and salt free. A SEAL platoon might start a mission by jumping from a helicopter or an airplane into the water, or swimming ashore from a boat. For a mission that requires an extended stay in a harsh climate, we must ensure that water, whether from the ocean, a stream, or rain, does not soak the clothing that will keep us warm and alive. Either way, we are getting wet and carrying gear that must not get wet.

To keep our gear dry, we have bags made of waterproof cloth or plastic with watertight zippers. A little thing like neglecting to put grease on the zipper or allowing corrosion to creep along it can degrade its ability to deny water entry to the important stuff. After two hours in the water, a small leak can soak a man's clothes and render radios or other essential gear inoperable. Not maintaining a seemingly little thing like a zipper can compromise the success of a mission!

Although the bags are extremely durable, they can still be punctured. The "dry bags" have nozzles on them. To check for leaks, a man simply blows a dry bag up and rotates it in a pan of water, the same way you'd test a bike tire for a leak. This entire process takes about five minutes if you're being thorough. But skipping this vital check can waste days of planning and gear preparation, thousands of dollars of aviation fuel (if you've been inserted by air), countless man-hours, your unit's reputation, and possibly somebody's life, depending on what gear is ruined.

SEALs have learned these lessons over time and passed them down. And this is why every SEAL maintains a log of lessons learned and consults it regularly. Something may seem so obvious that it can never be forgotten. But it can, and at the most inopportune time. Record lessons learned and prevent catastrophe.

Great leaders are vigilant. The achievement of Team goals is paramount, and as the leader of the Team you must be looking one step ahead of the action and encouraging your Team to do the same. Focus on the task at hand, but be aware of potential future stumbling points.

You must maintain a vigilant stance in order to prevent problems that could disturb the smooth and proper functioning of your Team and the flow of its members' routines when they're working toward Team goals. This is not restricted to machinery and procedures. It includes the care of your Team. It is a grave mistake to wait for problems to occur before dealing with them. People have emotions, concerns, interests, and families outside of the workplace. While it would be ideal if nothing personal entered the professional world, such an expectation is unrealistic. An employee with a sick family member may not show signs of distress, but they will be there—and they will affect the work that individual is able to perform for himself and for the Team. Do not be afraid of being human. Although there may not be anything you can do directly, a simple "How is your father doing?" could be the one nice gesture of the day that helps this person feel that he is indeed part of a Team that cares and, more importantly, that his leader is concerned about him.

People are often reluctant to get too personal or are concerned that they might ask the wrong questions. They fear that they may cause offense or aggravate the problem by talking about it. Honest concern does not hurt people; isolation does. When someone has a difficult problem, the simple expression and acknowledgment that you know something is bothering him and are available to help may be enough to prevent the demoralization he might suffer if he were left to feel isolated and alone. This is not to suggest that you seek out every detail of his problem, only that you let him know that he is a part of a Team that is concerned about its members.

Handle looming issues before they become a problem. The cohesion and integrity of the Team must come first. If non-Team players and self-interest plague your organization, you will not be able to foster the Team spirit necessary to survive. It must be known that you expect everyone to act and work as a Team. If you want to run a strong Team, this is not a rule that can be broken. There will be personality conflicts. The vigilant leader will notice these festering and deal with them before they get out of control. Your Team members don't need to like each other; they just need to know that you expect them to put their differences aside while at work. If they are unable to do so, counsel them, document it, and carry on with business.

You cannot identify a downward trend if you don't know what the trend is in the first place. How can you notice when Team members are having problems if you are engrossed with your own tasks? To be an effective leader, you will need to learn the art of dynamic interaction with people and develop a far-reaching and innovative vision. Being involved means knowing when issues arise, identifying when Team members are having problems, and expressing the fact that you are their leader and are resolute that these problems be taken care of. This might mean that you refer them to your human resources department or simply give them the moral support of your interest. You are the custodian of the Team and believe in it.

Never leave a man behind! This is and has been the keystone of the success of the Navy SEALs. Dead or alive, bloody or broken, Team members—all of them—are coming home! It is their resolute confidence in this fact that makes SEALs willing to go so far over the edge and into harm's way for the well-being of the Team. Before operations,

Team members make sure that everyone is part of the planning, the work, and the preparation of a successful mission. No one wants to put a Teammate into a risky situation unnecessarily, so every individual makes sure that he takes care of himself, to prevent his Teammates from having to go back in to get him. All Team members, at the same time, are willing to go back into a risky situation to get out a Teammate who was such a great part of their personal and professional development and success.

SEALs do everything as a Team. In competition, men seek to push, motivate, and improve their Teammates. On liberty, in a live-fire training exercise, or in a real-world operation, the attitude is the same: The welfare and safety of the Team is paramount to personal gain.

In a real-world firefight, you must win the fight before beginning your rescue efforts. It may appear that getting everyone home is not the top priority, and at that point it is not. The goal is and must be to win the fight. If you do not have fire superiority, rescue efforts will only produce more casualties. The fact remains, however, that come hell or high water, and whether it takes one hour or three days, SEALs will get everyone home.

Your Teammates must arrive each day secure in the knowledge that they are going to be taken care of. They must be allowed to work without worrying about whether someone else will take credit for their labor. They must be secure in the knowledge that their Teammates will not take advantage or purposely benefit from another Teammate's misfortune. This *trust* is integral to the success and cohesion of SEALs and can be for your Team. Trust and confidence in Teammates prevents problems—from the impossibility of collaboration for fear of exploitation to isolation when dealing with personal problems.

## What Makes a SEAL

Although there are no recipes for what makes a SEAL, there are two primary common factors:

### *Dedication to a Mission or Goal Beyond Oneself*

This is, in fact, a common trait among all servicemen and -women—Army, Navy, Air Force, Marines, and Coast Guard. It is the willingness to put a common goal before personal interest. The common goal is national defense. The vast majority of people who join the military are willing to work long, grueling hours for little money, to be away from home and family for months on end, and to put themselves in harm's way to defend the freedom and rights of people they do not know. A common goal and a sense of purpose—this is the power of the Team concept! The men and women of our armed forces view the country as a Team and the citizens as its members. They don't like everyone, agree with everyone, or even know everyone, but they perform their military duties because it is the right thing to do and in the best interest of the Team!

In the Navy SEALs you will find a corps of men of the highest caliber with unwavering resolve and dedication to duty and country. This is not to say that SEALs are all from the same mold—quite the contrary. SEALs are electrical engineers, plumbers, nurses, and microbiologists. Rhodes scholars work alongside those who hold only a simple high school degree. Some were reared in the hills of West Virginia and some in the most affluent settings society has to offer.

In your organization, you want and need steadfast commitment and dedication to the Team on the part of each Team member—and their refusal to quit no matter what! You must build, support, and defend a solid corps of employees—full- and part-time, and temporary—who believe in and have a vested interest in the success of the Team. You cannot do this as part of an isolated elitist hierarchy. If your Team sees you as an overbearing, unapproachable recluse, you will merely have people working a job, not a Team of motivated personnel moving together toward a common goal. Sense the climate and adjust accordingly.

## Fear of Failure and of Not Giving One's All to the Team

This drives every SEAL! You know that the men with you will give every ounce of energy, and then some, for you and for the others around them. If you fail your Team, you fail yourself. When part of a Team, the worst feeling you can have is that when your Team needed you the most, you did not come through. The opposite, of course, is the deep feeling of satisfaction for not only a job well done but also the knowledge that you and every one of your Teammates have benefited.

This is the key to any truly successful Team. You cannot force this feeling of duty and dedication on someone; it needs to come from them. You must trust every individual on your Team, and they must trust you. Tolerance of anything less will be harmful to your Team. Ethical issues must be handled swiftly, confidentially, and fairly. People cannot focus on the task at hand and the common goal if they are constantly fearful that someone may undermine their efforts or steal their accomplishments.

## Team Tips

### Encourage Physical and Mental Fitness

A person in good physical and mental condition is less likely to get sick and miss work. They are apt to be productive longer and will maintain a more positive self-image. Exercise gives people time to think, relieves stress, and simply gets a person's blood flowing. Those in good physical condition will be more productive during working hours. SEALs in staff positions and support personnel attached to a SEAL Team are allotted time for physical training (P.T.) every morning because it makes them sharper throughout the day and stronger in the long run. The standards are high, and so are the levels of performance and the results. This is maintenance of the body and mind and must not be overlooked. Allotting time for fitness will pay dividends.

## Preventive Maintenance Is Simplicity

Little things you do now prevent large issues later. You must raise the standards of weaker Team members and never force your hot runners to degrade their high standards to accommodate the less motivated.

While I was in ROTC, we were required to attend P.T. three mornings per week. After the first week, several of us asked that the sessions be made more challenging. The answer came back: no. When we inquired why, the answer was that the staff was concerned that if they made the P.T. sessions too hard, the new midshipmen would become discouraged and quit.

After a few months the physical conditioning of the new members of the unit had not improved, and the morale of the physically fit had degraded. In this particular case, the decisions of the administration had prevented maintenance! The lack of vision and strong goals got the young midshipmen stuck. These new men perceived that they were unable to achieve—after months of "work" they had not seen improvement. This problem took the entire next semester to fix.

## *Risk Assessment*

Risk assessment is simply seeking out all the information about what your Team faces and determining your ability to deal with those issues. Almost every SEAL training exercise and mission is high risk. Operations may involve parachuting, rifle and pistol fire, explosives training, scuba diving, jumping from or being suspended from a helicopter, and more. While exciting, all these operations and training missions must be undertaken with the utmost professionalism, or lives will be lost.

To prevent as many mishaps as possible, SEALs use and maintain risk-assessment sheets, which are filled in and scrutinized before each evolution. These sheets detail, the experience level of the participants, the difficulty of the task, environmental conditions, the nature of the operation, the equipment to be used, and the physical and mental state of the participants. Other things, as well, are listed on the sheet; these can encompass anything the men feel is pertinent. The experience and wisdom of risk assessment is geared entirely to the prevention of mishaps and accidents. Strict adherence to the usage of risk-assessment sheets has greatly reduced the number of training incidents within the Teams.

As SEALs, we pride ourselves on our extremely low accident rate. A risk assessment includes the completion of supervisor checks. Before any diving, shooting, demolition, or air operation, each Team receives at least two checks from certified supervisors, who undergo a rigorous training and qualification process for their specialties. These are apart from the self- and buddy checks SEALs continually perform and receive from Teammates. We are extremely serious about our preoperational checks and never skip or deride them, because they prevent accidents and save lives. As a Team, we have a vested interest in the health and welfare of every Team member. When the jumpmaster slaps the back of your parachute and tells you you are good to go, you know you are. You have faith that even if you do not get along socially, as Teammates you will never allow harm to befall one another. That is the beauty of a solid and successful Team.

## Keep People Dedicated to and Confident in the Team Concept

Be involved from the start. This will keep you from having to play catch-up later. If your Team knows you believe in the Team, they will believe in you.

## Keep People Informed

Share your vision with the Team. Let them know where they are going. Let them share in your vision and enthusiasm. Giving your Team information and insight into your plans prevents frustration and confusion.

Before I was the platoon point man, I was rear security, the last guy in the patrol, and the farthest from the plan. It could be frustrating at times to be in the back with no idea about what was going on up front.

Lesson learned! When I became point man, I would, if the situation permitted, make my way around the platoon during stops to bring the guys up to speed on what was going on. I would tell them how far we had gone, where we were, any plan changes, and what to expect next. Not only did this make them feel more a part of the action, but it gave them valuable information to use in a crisis or when the platoon got split up or if the decision makers were shot. The feedback I got afterward was great. The simple effort it took to tell people what was going on made a huge difference to them. They felt informed and included, and their curiosity was satisfied.

## Chapter 9 Lessons

➤ A vigilant leader is an informed leader.

➤ Isolation can allow people to feel demoralized and become and distant.

➤ Invest the time in preventive maintenance now to avoid wasting time later.

➤ Record lessons learned to prevent catastrophes.

➤ Be interested in your Team members; ask them how they are doing.

➤ Keep people informed to prevent the frustration of "not knowing."

# CHAPTER 10
## *The Four Links*

It is your responsibility as the leader and controller of the Team to ensure that the accepted perception (which is your Team's reality) is consistent with the system and vision you have conceived and set in motion for the Team. Everything from innocent misinformation to malicious distortion of the facts for personal gain can affect your Team and its ability to achieve your objectives. You must keep your people informed as often and thoroughly as possible. If your Team has the facts and the details, they will not need to look to outside sources for information or, worse, believe made-up details for a sense of fulfillment. When you keep your Team abreast of current events, you diminish much of the power of the rumor network.

The concept of "close hold"—keeping your Team close-knit and self-sufficient—encompasses both the security and the sanctity of the Team as well as the ideals and environment you have chosen to foster. Build a Team that is self-sufficient and steadfast in the pursuit of the common vision and stay vigilant in your protection and direction of that vision.

The very concept of a Team suggests that there is a common tie or thread that binds people together in the pursuit of familiar goals. In times of difficulty or uncertainty, people will turn to what is most known and comfortable. These aspects of Team membership—sanctity and camaraderie—must not be overlooked or undervalued. These, in fact, are Team advantages you must capitalize on.

We are social creatures and need interaction with groups of people who are like-minded, who have a sense of common duty or similar goals, or whom we wish to emulate. Teams provide friendship, security, assistance, and a sense of belonging. They also meet a variety of other social and emotional needs. For some, the Team is the extension of family; for others, it is the group or entity with which they identify, made up of people whom they simply enjoy being around and involved with.

The attitude you maintain while building, developing, and leading your Team will greatly affect you and the other members of the Team. Your Team will be what you make of it, and the easiest way to identify its needs and the needs of its members is to hone your skills of introspection and determine what qualities you expect of a Team. What is it that you look for in a Team? Are there some aspects of a Team you find more desirable than others? Think about past group experiences and draw from those memories and lessons learned to improve your current situation.

We must accept that the world is a dynamic laboratory, yet remain resolute in our determination to manipulate our environment for the good of our Team and ourselves rather than let it control us. You must take ownership and be in command of what you can control, learn to leave the rest, and avoid fruitless entanglements. The true essence of leadership is the calculated, moral, and thoughtful organization of your world. Your responsibility as a leader is to mold, maintain, and develop your Team and the environment in which it works.

In times of change or when the environment becomes hostile or the terrain difficult, the Team must be where your people go for comfort. It must be the source your people turn to for help, motivation, and inspiration. When a Team is properly maintained, it achieves a success that builds on itself. The SEALs I have had the honor of serving with cherish and look forward to showing up for work each day, even when the training schedule is grueling. Their overwhelming sense of duty, accomplishment, and belonging arises not from numbers but from safety in security. They know their platoon mates would risk their own lives and well-being if anyone on the Team were in trouble or needed assistance.

There is consolation in the knowledge that if you have a problem, you can turn to your Teammates for answers and need not worry about the information being leaked or becoming the topic of gossip. It is unrealistic to expect that no one will ever complain or be dissatisfied with their jobs. It is your job and duty, however, to ensure that when they do have issues, they rely on the solid, supportive Team. If there is the perception, correct or not, that they cannot count on your support, then you have failed at one of your most important tasks as a leader: the foundation and preservation of a sturdy, loyal, and available support network. If your people have concerns, you must take the time to find out what the issues really are. That is your job, your responsibility; it is a duty you assume when you accept a leadership position. You cannot use the excuse that you have no time. At the very minimum, you must gain the pertinent knowledge and assign someone you trust to handle the problem.

You do not want your people looking to outside sources for support or comfort. Handle as many problems as possible internally. Your people must see the strength of the Team. If they feel that you have breached confidentiality on sensitive issues, or have treated those issues with insincerity or as trivial matters, you will lose your edge. In short, it is imperative that you remain open to your Team, for it is when they feel that you do not care that they turn elsewhere. This lack of communication can be particularly detrimental.

Deal with issues internally whenever possible. It is not appropriate to release information without the consent of your Team. If you must reveal a situation you observed in your Team in order to facilitate important lessons learned, you can do so, but you must make the facts clear and concise so as not to mislead or cloud the truth.

Different communities and jobs have their own jargon, which can sound foreign or confusing to outsiders. This can create a grave misconception, which can lead to unwarranted reactions and tainted images. This perception can then become reality. Consider the young recruit calling home. He tells his mother that he had a rough day and the instructor made him "beat his face." The mother reacts in horror, imagining her bloodied son on the other end of the telephone. Because she doesn't know that "beat your face" simply means to do push-ups, she now has a distorted and negative view of the instructor—and the military!

The possibilities for miscommunication increase when dealing with issues of greater magnitude. Study language to become a more effective communicator. Identifying the nuances of language used in different communities, organizations, companies, and groups brings to light the rapidity with which the intention and meaning of oral communication can be misconstrued. When talking to those outside of your Team, make sure you explain the details in standard English to avoid the misconception of jargon.

## The Four Links

Comfort in sanctity!

Sanctity in trust!

Trust in security!

Security in the Team!

The four links of cohesion are fundamental and crucial to the survival of a Team. If any of these are breached or tainted, you have squandered a portion of a link or an entire one, which may lead to the compromise of Team integrity. Recently, the collapse of several major corporations and a host of midsized and small companies resulted from this chain being broken. Those who held the leadership roles violated and exploited the trust the Team had in them. They left people behind—their own employees, their investors, those who held their companies' stocks in 401Ks and other retirement accounts, and, in some instances, the American taxpayer.

If, in a leadership position, you plan to deceive your Team, you willfully sacrifice your honor. The members of a Team look to their leader for wisdom and guidance, and they trust that a leader will take care of them. The maligned, self-righteous leader is a treacherous entity and has no place on a Team. The mere presence of such an individual destroys all that they might have achieved by their personal vision. Hold the four links in high regard and maintain them, preventive action being the most advantageous. Remain in tune with the condition of the links and keep them strong.

*Comfort in sanctity* stems from the level of solace that one finds when they know that their partners sustain the same reverence for the fundamental operation and framework of the Team. People seek membership in those groups with which they can identify. It follows that if they are secure in the knowledge that they are among like-minded people or people who hold similar goals and ambitions dear, they will experience a greater sense of comfort.

*Sanctity in trust.* Once you have identified the group that reveres the same ideals and practices, you will form a bond. The notion of sanctity in trust is an internal ethic. Personal standards must be genuine in each member. One person who lacks resolve can destroy the natural strength of an experienced Team and decimate a fledgling one. Those who would violate the trust of another must not be allowed to remain on the Team.

*Trust in security.* With like-minded people who sustain the veneration of trust, you, as the leader, must ensure that the security they now feel is not debased. The Team has developed through the first two steps naturally. As the leader, you are ever mindful of situations or issues that could potentially discredit the secure boundaries of your Team. You cannot detach yourself from the Team and become distant. In accepting the leadership role, you relinquished the luxury of deniability. You cannot say, "Well, it wasn't my responsibility," because when you're the person in charge, everything is! If a junior Team member screws up, you had better believe that the eyes of scrutiny will be cast upon the senior member. This is a fact of leadership and a burden you must be willing to bear. The overall security and integrity of the Team is in your hands, and you must protect it.

*Security in the Team.* The recognition of like ideals is coupled with a belief in trust. You are the omnipresent provider of Team security and integrity! After your Team has achieved the first three links, the entire group will move into the final stage: security in the Team. You are now at the point where the like-minded members of the Team have gelled as a group and have identified the fact that you, their leader, are the bastion of Team integrity. But in a subtle and sure movement from personality-based leadership to Team-oriented duty and responsibility, Team members now come to the Team for support. They will bring you that new and great idea and look to you to choose Team members to evaluate, improve, and implement good ideas. They will count on you to maintain close hold of that information. But when they have personal problems, they know they can count on the Team to do everything within reason to lessen the severity of their misfortune. That is what being on a Team is all about!

## Preventing a Break in the Links

### Rumor and Gossip

You cannot tolerate maligned rumor or gossip on the part of any Team member, and you certainly can't participate yourself. People will talk about other people—that is human nature. It is not your job to weasel around the breakroom sniffing out every little story. That is neither effective nor appropriate.

Your best approach to stifling destructive rumors is to prevent them in the first place. Fostering a strong Team atmosphere and providing timely information are your most effective tools. When people feel left behind or in the dark, they start to talk. Their natural curiosity or need to know will surface. Since they are not getting information from the leader, they will try to solve the mystery of lack of information among themselves. Theories will filter through the workplace, and soon it will be hard for people to tell truth from fiction.

Not all information is suitable for mass consumption. You must use your discretion when determining what information the Team needs and what must be kept from them. At other times, there will be no need to tell the Team anything. When there is vital information that affects the Team, however, you must inform all concerned as soon as possible.

See that every situation is handled at the lowest possible level. There are certain situations that not everybody needs to know about. Inform your Team about the type of situations you want to be notified of. You don't need to know that Joe is out of printer ink, but you do need to know if he was just in an automobile accident. When I was new to the Teams, I was determined to do everything right. I attacked every task with a zealous fervor and reported to my chief promptly upon completion. After a few months he stopped me, saying that he really didn't need to hear every detail of every second of every day because he had a lot of things to do besides listen to me report. I said, "Roger that, Chief. What do you want to know?" He looked at me with a grin and replied, "As long as I'm not gonna get shotgunned on the carpet in front of the skipper, I don't need to know about it."

He wanted to know about issues that might concern people by virtue of their severity. Getting "shotgunned" means having someone grill you about something you should know about but don't. "On the carpet" means standing in front of the commanding officer in his office . . . usually with the door shut. "Skipper" is just another term to refer to the commanding officer. If the chief wasn't going to have to deal with it, he didn't need to know about it.

What does and doesn't—and what should or shouldn't—get reported is unique to each organization. The amount of information required by the leadership is often a function of time, the situations at hand, and the decisions to be made. Planning long-range strategy demands a different type and amount of information than making sure an angry customer gets satisfaction. Give your working leaders the tools to exercise information triage and weed out what you don't need to or want to know about. You will need to set the stage for your Team and explain what you expect from them.

## Malicious or Inadvertent Spreading of Sensitive Information

If all events of the day become immediate public knowledge, there can be serious fallout. This is especially important when dealing with counseling and personal issues. Confidentiality concerning evaluations is paramount. If you counseled an individual about a potentially damaging issue and promised to keep it confidential, it must remain just that. You cannot use it against them later, ever. If you are unable to make that commitment, do not make the guarantee.

Before you talk to someone about sensitive information, determine their need to know. Make sure that everyone on the Team understands this principle. Unscrupulous individuals sometimes utilize others' deeply personal or private information for their own gain. These people, who violate the Team's trust in order to improve their own status, are a thorn in the side of any organization and must not be tolerated.

We have already discussed the vast importance of security. In addition to the controlled release of information, you must consider the leadership's capacity to deal with specific issues. A minor infraction taken straight to the top may lead to a perception that the offense is of a greater magnitude than it really is. Furthermore, the leader is faced with the prospect of solving the problem. The choices are to send it back down the chain of command or deal with it. It is important that if issues arrive at your desk without having gone through the proper chain of command, you send them back to the beginning. If you allow people to skip their leadership, you set your Team up for failure.

Stress the necessity of handling issues at the lowest level. This ensures that all concerned are informed, and it relieves you from having to deal with the small day to day happenings. A breach of the chain of command sends a damaging signal that the Team lacks structure. People need and desire structure, the lack of which can ruin a great Team or prevent it from ever developing.

Make the necessity for discretion and confidentiality perfectly clear to the Team leadership and every member of the Team. How you handle sensitive information will affect the lives of your people, the development of your subordinates, and the success of your Team. You cannot treat serious, personal matters as a joke or allow them to become the subject of gossip. You cannot tolerate such behavior from your Team.

The security your Team provides its members is the greatest asset you have in any organization. To neglect the maintenance of that comfort or to allow it to be subverted by rumors and deceit is the mark of bad, irresponsible leadership. When I was a boy and had done something wrong, my father would sit me down before doling out my punishment. He would explain my infraction and suggest that in the future, before I acted upon my boyish instincts, I should apply the "reasonable-man test": If you are doing something, or about to, and it does not feel right, stop and think. If it seems wrong to release information, it probably is. The exploitation of information for personal gain is definitely wrong. Be proactive and vigilant in your role as a leader. This is your Team, and it is your responsibility to keep close hold of it.

# Chapter 10 Lessons

➤ Close hold is about confidentiality as well as the maintenance of the ideals and foundation of the Team.

➤ A degraded or missing fundamental link defiles the Team and will prevent it from operating as a Team.

➤ Teams are based on comfort in security, not safety in numbers.

➤ Control damaging rumors by keeping your Team and those concerned informed in a timely manner.

➤ Support your Team's chain of command and let it work by backing your leadership and their decisions.

➤ When in a quandary about what to do or who needs to know what, apply the "reasonable-person test."

➤ Do not lose control of your Team through the inappropriate dissemination of information.

# Chapter 11
## *Teammates, Not Lackeys*

Even the best-trained and most highly motivated people require structure. Any group of men and women working together, regardless of their experience, will still need a chain of command. That chain must be strong and provide the rest of the Team with the comfort of knowing that their leadership and support structures will work and be there for them. Leeway for the individual to act, to be empowered to make decisions and critical changes while working to achieve goals, is not only necessary but beneficial to the growth of both the individual and the Team. But too much latitude can be detrimental. If you have a mixed group of new and experienced Team members, those with more training and know-how must set the example at *all* times. If they don't, your new Teammates may not have the mental, physical, or emotional resources and direction to draw upon when faced with important tasks. But this training by example will also be important when the new people later become the mentors for the Team.

The men of the Naval Special Warfare community are unique among the military ranks for several reasons. U.S. Navy SEALs, officers and enlisted men alike, go through the same training, side by side. There is no difference between the training officers and enlisted men receive. From this a common tie is drawn. It is much easier for a SEAL officer to relate to and understand what his men are going through because he has done or is doing the same thing. Officers are afforded certain accoutrements, privileges, and extra work in conjunction with their rank, yet they are aware of what their men experience and are conscious of the ramifications of their decisions. The relationship between SEAL officers and enlisted personnel soon becomes one of mutual understanding, support, and complement. Officers do not exploit their men, and the men watch out for and take care of their officers. The officers treat the men with the utmost respect, demand the utmost from the men, and in turn get the very best from the Team.

Anyone who varies from this code of conduct will soon find himself drummed out of the corps for not being a Team player. This includes men who act selfishly, who strive to achieve their own goals rather than the Team's, and who are micromanagers, complainers, or gossips. Every man must carry his own weight, as well as the weight of every member of the Team, at all times. No Team member is ever left behind.

Before I executed my orders to BUD/S, I worked for an officer in the regular Navy who took glee in wallowing in what he perceived to be his own greatness. While working for this man, I wasted countless hours performing tasks required mostly because of his own ego. Tedious busywork filled every gap in each already packed workday.

At the same time, this officer kept everything we had to accomplish a secret and acted as if we didn't need to know anything. He was outwardly arrogant and unwilling to admit when he was in error. It was obvious that everything he did was geared toward making himself look better. He would often claim others' successes as his own. And when he thought there was even a chance that something would make him look bad, without hesitation he would point a finger at someone else. He would do or say anything to make someone else take the burden for his shortfalls.

Even worse, the men and women in his command had pressing personal issues that needed attention. On countless occasions, his subordinates (including me) would fill in the proper paperwork for personal requests and forward them through the proper channels, only to have him deny them outright. He denied my first five requests to attend BUD/S. He said it would reflect poorly on his retention numbers.

People like this may enjoy the outward appearance of success, at least in the eyes of their superiors, for a short time. But this kind of selfishness always catches up to them. This officer wound up with the lowest reenlistment record for his personnel among his fellow officers. He had rocketed up the chain of command, only to lose the confidence of his men and women, and then his command and his career.

This is a vital example of why it is crucial that you take charge of your organization and mold it into a hotbed of motivation, creativity, and ideas. The way you develop and support your Team will have a profound effect on the junior and advancing personnel in your organization and will influence both the longevity and the quality of your Team. This, in turn, will directly affect the tasks they have to do and the goals they have to achieve in the years to come.

It is important to develop and maintain an experienced group, or training cell, for the purpose of instructing and preparing new Team members. Every Team has its own idiosyncrasies, regardless of the tasks and goals involved, and it is much more efficient to teach new people how a Team works than to wait for them to learn on their own. You need to inform new arrivals of everything you can to get them started on a solid footing, and then you must watch to make sure they are able to ask questions and feel comfortable doing so.

Your training cell will consist of trusted individuals who have proven to be effective and productive role models and mentors. Effectiveness goes much further than just high productivity; an effective training-cell leader brings with him or her the entire package. A person can be highly productive at their job yet lack the leadership traits necessary to develop and train people. This is of critical importance. When you establish a proper training cell, it forms the vital first impressions a new member gets of the Team, and it will frequently set the stage for that new member's development. The members of the training cell should be the people who have the best mix of intelligence, knowledge of the Team and its goals, and ability to form solid interpersonal relationships. Your investment in your new Teammates will become your profit, and the Team's, in the future.

You should not do away with the rites of passage or remove the duties of the junior personnel. To do so could adversely affect morale. There must be a natural maturation process. You must properly indoctrinate junior members into the Team. If they are privy to your Team's high standards and are part of the Team's success up front, they will be more motivated and dedicated to their own development.

The goal of great leaders is to provide an atmosphere where Team members motivate themselves and govern their actions for the good and well-being of the whole. People who get treated by you or other Team members as lackeys will be of little importance in the long run. Teammates are assets to be developed and supported; ideally, they will be productive and satisfied members of a winning and successful organization. Teammates will support and protect you, whereas lackeys will let you fall!

At my second SEAL Team I was entrusted with the duty of running the training cell's land warfare department. I was the senior enlisted person in the chain of command concerning land warfare tactics development and scheduling and training of the platoons preparing to deploy. I was still new to high-profile leadership positions and was determined not to treat any member of my Team as a lackey or a gofer. I consulted my lessons-learned book and combed it for the leadership glitches of others I had witnessed in my time in the Navy. One of my highlighted notes was about servile labor without adequate information about purpose or goal. I promised myself that my men would be informed, efficiently worked, well trained, and encouraged to become self-motivated. I pored over training schedules, made revisions, and assigned people tasks that fit their expertise. I took on my share of the work as a functioning member of my Team.

Almost all of the men working for me in my training cell had more experience than I did, and I was in charge by virtue of my rank. Other elements highlighted in my lessons-learned log dealt with effective leadership skills I had seen in my time in the Navy. Leaders who'd gotten their hands dirty with the other men in order to foster unity and to pass on valuable knowledge had set a powerful example. Leaders I'd admired were already present in the morning when we showed up, and they were still there when the men went home for the day. I wanted to be that kind of leader.

But in my efforts to be the "superleader" I neglected to consider the mountain of paperwork and other duties associated with my new position. And I still had training to complete in order to be effective at my job. In short, I had not yet made the full transition from worker to leader. I had taken on too much.

At the same time, we were understaffed and I was determined not to overwork my men. After a couple months of my whirlwind schedule, my staff approached me. They asked if we could all sit down and talk. I was exhausted and in need of sleep, but I always made time for my men, so the six of us sat down together. They said they felt I was taking on too much work and not giving them enough. I realized then that I had been obsessed and overzealous in my pursuit of developing a strong and satisfied Team.

One of the guys looked at me and said, "Hey, you need to concentrate on your job and delegate more tasks to us—we're getting too much sleep." We all laughed, but I got the point. We talked for the next hour, and I started doling out new assignments. It was a great feeling to have my men care that much for their jobs, the success of the mission, and me—and I was pleased that they'd taken the time to talk to me about it. I was also glad that I had worked for great leaders who had always taken the time to listen to me, so that I'd afforded my men the same right.

Later that evening when I was in bed, getting ready to drift off to sleep, I reflected on the day. I was elated at the performance of my Team. It was then that the true spirit and effectiveness of a great Team became evident. I had gone overboard to ensure that they were happy and taken care of, so when it became apparent that I was overworking myself, they'd come to me to resolve the issue. It had been obvious to them that my interest was in their well-being and the success of the Team and its mission: the training of war fighting platoons. Had I not been an ardent proponent of the Team experience, they would have most likely let me work myself into failure. They had not. I'd made mistakes with good intentions, wanting only the betterment of the Team. And my Team had taken care of me.

That is the beauty of a solidly founded and cooperative organization. The members of your Team are the future of your Team. You cannot treat your Teammates like lackeys or you will have transcended the boundaries of leadership and slipped back into the role of a manager. Members of a highly effective and successful Team cooperate among themselves and share a common purpose. Avoid throwing your Team into jobs without providing them with the connection to the completion of goals. You cannot afford to have your Team undertake seemingly fruitless labor. Inform them when you can, and they will understand when you cannot.

In your organization you are sure to have young people fresh out of college bristling with idealism and knowledge. That is a wonderful and necessary asset, but it does not replace or compare to the knowledge and practice of experienced employees. A college degree is indicative of trainability, well-roundedness, and a thirst for knowledge. These qualities combined with the real-world experience of loyal employees can be powerful tools, not only for the achievement of Team goals but for your professional development and that of your Team members. Entrust the core of experienced employees with managing the fundamental operation of the workforce. Let the new members infuse the work environment with enthusiasm, energy, and excitement about the tasks at hand, and encourage them to provide new perspectives on routine tasks. Your job is to train future leaders, not to wring the life out of subordinates.

How you handle them will be how they handle their subordinates in the future.

You must be visible, interested, and vigilant. Your vision, and that of your Team, will include the outlook and mission of your organization. Share with your Team the big picture and the experience of longevity. Make it obvious that they are not toiling for a paycheck; rather, they are producing a foundation upon which the vision of the Team will stand. Mutual respect is not merely vital but necessary if you and your Team are to succeed.

## Chapter 11 Lessons

➢ The goal of a Team is to develop its members, not work them into submission.

➢ Involve the Team in the attainment of goals by keeping them informed.

➢ If you respect and support your Team, they will revere and protect you.

➢ Mutual respect is paramount.

# CHAPTER 12
## *What Is Expected from You*

Survival in today's business world demands a shift from the old paradigm of managerial "leadership" to that of true leadership. It is no longer enough to run a tight ship and do what is expected of you. You need to be out front, leading your Team to victory by direction and example. A Team will expect its leader to set goals and standards, see that they are met, and follow through with decisions affecting the Team. Your Team members need you to fill that role and perform well. When you provide your Team with the solid leader they require, you are doing your job. You have the latitude to adapt, change, revamp, and customize your style. Your options are limitless, within reason, and afford you the opportunity to effect real change in your organization and its future.

Until now, everything in this book has been geared toward helping you learn to control your environment, develop your Team, and maintain it. Now is the time to think about what your Team members need and expect from you. One does not become a great leader by virtue of time spent in the trenches. Having been a member of the workforce prior to coming into a leadership position is by no means a guarantee of success. The information and experiences you have gained can only be as useful and beneficial as your application of them to your present

117

situation and your long-term goals. If you choose to ignore vital lessons learned, you choose to fail.

Reflect for a moment on the leaders you have known in your past. Write down their names; next to each name, identify that person as a good or a bad leader. Now annotate the list further: Were they poor or exceptional? Identify the qualities, or lack thereof, that made them so, in your opinion. Ask yourself what you needed in a leader at that time in your life. What do you need now? I encourage you to use these notes to draw up a quick matrix. List names on one axis and good and bad qualities on the other. Reflect on all the details you can remember to obtain a fair assessment of each person.

Now that you have refreshed your notion of the qualities of good and bad leaders, I am willing to bet that some of the traits you found in your exceptional leaders were confidence, knowledge, and forthrightness. On the bad side, you might have listed arrogance, lack of vision, and narrow-mindedness. Apply these standards to yourself, assessing your own leadership. Does your self-evaluation match your Team's perception of you?

While you can't know exactly what others think of you, you can, through this self-evaluation, determine what you think of your leadership skills and what kind of leader you think you are. But be careful. You might ask, "What is expected of me?" and answer, "I am in charge! I'm the one who should be doing all the expecting!" This self-righteous and elitist attitude will increase the risk of your alienating your people. If you have acted or managed this way in the past, you may find that an ineffective and divisive "us against them" attitude exists in your workplace. If your Team members have the perception that they cannot trust you, they will not be willing to go that extra mile when you need it the most. Begin today to rectify the situation by acting and leading in a way that says that the Team—which encompasses its well-being and the well-being and professional development of its members, including you—is the most important aspect of your workplace. Your Team members will work for you. But you must fulfill your responsibility. The coach may be the head of the Team, but he or she is nonetheless part of that Team.

You must let your Team know that you will be there, in one way or another, if they truly need help. In all matters, personal and professional, your Team members must feel that they can count on one another. For example, if there is a death in someone's family, that person must know that you will give them time to take care of family matters. The rest of the team must *want* to pick up the slack, knowing that if they were in the same situation, the Team would do the same thing for them. If you advocate and promote a strong Team atmosphere, it will begin to build on itself. Your Team members will see that you have their interests in mind, and you will find that when you need help, the Team is there for you. The results you will get from a Team wanting to help will be tenfold over those of a group of people begrudgingly meeting a deadline.

When your Team members perceive that the person in charge of their livelihood is strong-willed and confident, it puts the entire organization at ease. The security you provide allows your Team members to concentrate on their jobs instead of wondering how they will put food on the table or whether you will support their needs as they work for Team goals. Lack of confidence in a leader is disconcerting. A Milquetoast and passive demeanor inspires nothing but doubt about whether the leader will be able to stand up for the Team when difficult issues arise.

It is not required that a Team leader be expert in every aspect of every job within the organization. It is imperative, however, that you have a thorough enough working knowledge to be able to communicate intelligently with your Team, both in the conduct of day-to-day business and for crisis management. If you come to them to solve a problem and cannot even speak about the issue, you're beginning with a deficit. The more you educate yourself, the more confident you will be around them. You will feel more in tune with them and better able to communicate. This is inspiring to them and crucial to your success.

You must pursue and acquire knowledge continuously, both about the inner workings of your Team, their jobs, and their personal needs, and about the environment in which you compete. Go to your people to learn. Often, they will know more about the competitive environment than you do—because they are on the front lines all the time. They expect you to use them for their wealth of knowledge, and when you do, it will do much for their morale.

Moreover, your Team members want to be challenged. If they are not, they will grow bored and listless. They will lose sight of the importance of the goals you have set and will perform their tasks competently but without enthusiasm, without wanting or feeling the need to excel. Your self-assurance must translate into confidence in your Team members, as a group and as individuals. You must have the confidence to let them take risks and allow them to break out. Sometimes they will succeed immediately. Most times, however, they will need to try and fail in order to eventually achieve success. As long as the result of this is the betterment of the individual and the Team, it is permissible and will move you toward your goals.

Members of a properly developed Team will invite challenge. They will look to you to encourage an environment of innovative and creative thinking. They will want to perform new tasks, regardless of the difficulty. They will learn everything they can, both from the Team and from outside resources, to effect their success in the task and the Team's success in achieving its goals.

But if you overly accommodate and appease your Team members' individual wants, it will be hard for your Team to respect and trust you. For instance, you must seriously consider it when a Team member wants to try to do a task with which they are not familiar. Their proper training will be your responsibility. But if you allow your Team members to do what they want without the proper knowledge, skills, and training, you will benefit neither the individual nor the Team.

By the same token, each member of the Team will have to take care of their own responsibilities before taking on new tasks or vying for time off or more flexible schedules.

At no time must one Team member perceive that they work harder or receive less than another—or that others are getting something for nothing. Each Team member must also hold dear the following principle: It is more important that the individual Team member pay attention to what they are doing and accomplishing rather than what they *think* the man or woman next to them is doing or getting. As in all things, you can facilitate this by being as open and free with information about Team efforts, goals, and achievements as possible. Praise the individual in front of the Team, but always make it clear that the Team has been integral and necessary for the individual's development.

Be straightforward and honest but tactful. Do not insult or demean people. Your Team needs you to be consistent and faithful to them and to the truth. The Team needs to know that you truly mean what you say. Euphemisms and passive language confuse and unseat your Team. Its leader must be stable and able to communicate without equivocation.

Preventive maintenance is the essence of simplicity. Little things you do now prevent large issues later. Raise the standards of the weaker, and never force your hot runners to degrade their high standards to accommodate less motivated Team members.

As I mentioned before, while in ROTC, I was required with the rest of the unit to attend physical training sessions three mornings per week. The sessions weren't challenging, and we requested tougher workouts. But the administration feared that this would turn some recruits away.

The members of the ROTC unit needed the senior members to be aggressive achievers and to challenge them. They needed motivation and incentive to do better during physical training. The instructors failed the Team, trying to achieve a short-term goal by coddling the weaker people. The administrators may have thought they were helping, but they perpetuated the weaker people's weaknesses.

The following semester I was placed in charge of physical training, and I fixed the problem. I offered the better-conditioned members a challenging regimen of exercise and encouraged the weaker folks to do as many perfect exercises as possible. It was more important that they do some repetitions perfectly than all of them poorly. This provided the maximum good for all concerned. The better-conditioned members had attainable goals to work for in the short term. The weaker, less physically conditioned people were able to see what they would eventually achieve. We all worked together. Everyone felt challenged and had great workouts without getting injured. The Team was able to concentrate on exercise because it was obvious to them that I had the knowledge to train them wisely. Before every new exercise I explained the correct way to execute it without damaging their bodies. This way they got stronger with less pain.

As I mentioned before, a complaining sailor is a happy sailor, and if he's not complaining, something is wrong. Think of it this way: If those working for you quietly and passively do their work, that is what you will get—quiet and passive action. On the other hand, consider a workforce not content with the norm and always open to and looking for a better way.

Your Team should avoid becoming obsessed with reinventing the wheel, but they must have the willingness to explore and develop ideas. Do not be afraid of change. What you may consider complaining could just be someone expressing a new, and quite possibly better, way of getting the job done. On the other hand, you need to quell unproductive bickering immediately. The entire Team will count on you (or the person you've assigned for this) to extinguish detrimental conflict in a timely and professional manner. Handle all disputes on the scene if possible. Leaving conflicts unaddressed tends to inflame opinion. If you enter into or notice a potentially or developed "hot" situation, determine whether it is appropriate to allow a cooling-off period. If your subordinate asks for a little time away from a situation, it is probably advisable to allow it. The Team depends on the preservation of order, and in this way, you can help provide it.

Chances are that some of your people will have put in more time in the workforce than you, depending on the type of work you do and your position within the organization. It is natural to feel slightly unworthy when put in charge of and tasked with leading those who have more experience. Training war-fighting platoons put me over men with more time in the Navy and of higher ranks than me. But I swallowed my selfish impulses and took the reins, thinking of the success of all involved. They didn't need a leader who was afraid of them; they needed one who held the goals and betterment of the Team and its members in the highest regard.

When you assume a leadership position, remember that someone chose you for the position and gave you the responsibility because they believed you could do it. Your responsibility is to step up to the challenge and take control of your environment—even when this is exceptionally difficult. Assess your situation and formulate your leadership plan. Create a strong vision and mission statement, and with these, set the stage. Act effectively and with conviction. Your Team expects and needs this from you. If you fail to take charge, your Team will not have confidence in you. Lead from the front with conviction and your Team will succeed.

# Chapter 12 Lessons

➤ Your Team requires that you:

1. Have confidence in your ability to lead.

2. Know enough about your organization to be able to speak about any potential issue. If something new arises, educate yourself immediately and handle it.

3. Be honest and forthright. Do not pull punches with your Team. They need you to be truthful and to the point.

➤ Experience is a part of, but not the only ingredient to, Team success. The Team needs your open-mindedness, confidence in their abilities, and respect. They need you to set strong goals and allow them the ability to achieve those goals.

# CONCLUSION:
## *Lessons Learned*

A Navy SEAL instructor gave the order "Forward march" through a bullhorn. Then he bellowed, "Everybody wants to be a Frogman on a sunny day!"

My entire BUD/S class linked arms and walked toward the crashing waves with apprehension. It was one o'clock in the morning, and we were already soaked and chilled to the bone. Those of us still shivering were the lucky ones. The ones who had transcended the boundary into hypothermia and exhaustion plodded forward in a near-catatonic state, too cold and battered to shiver any longer.

Ocean water splashed around my boots, then higher. The cold that came with it cut through my clothes, biting, slicing my skin like razor blades. We continued to shuffle forward until the water was knee-deep. "Halt!" bellowed the instructor through the bullhorn. "Taaaaaake seats!" The class collapsed into the water, arms solidly linked.

This had been our fifth trip to the surf zone that night; we were entering our fourth hour of sitting in the water. The instructors "requested" that we sing the theme song to *Gilligan's Island*—again! The words spilled out of our mouths as the waves contorted the line of men. Our arms wrenched with fatigue as we battled to keep them linked with those of the men next to us. If the chain broke, we'd earn more time in the water.

Our class leader, a former Marine Corps officer, yelled words of motivation and encouragement through numb, blue lips. To break our spirit, the instructors and their staff dissuaded this behavior, yet they privately admired his tenacity and leadership ethic.

Rip currents pulled the center of the class, and breakers pounded the ends, tearing at our ranks. The waves frequently interrupted my gaze, fixed as it was on the dark, featureless horizon. Immediately prior to impact, a mixed concert of mumblings warned of an incoming barrage of water. Hundreds of pounds of water smashed the class to the sandy bottom. Sandy water swirled around our heads, filling every orifice with salty grit.

The wave passed, and we collected ourselves to sit upright, arms still linked. Our abdominal muscles ached with tension as we fought to stay erect, closer to the precious oxygen provided by the air.

Thirty minutes later the lead instructor gave the orders that freed us from the icy, roaring ocean. He gathered the class in front of him, our arms still linked. "Everybody wants to be a Frogman on a sunny day," he said again. He and his men had wanted a quitter, but they didn't get one. The class and our Team spirit triumphed that night.

To some this may seem harsh treatment for any indoctrination or rite of passage. But "surf torture" is designed to test the will of prospective SEALs. The special operations profession is a game of high stakes in which men cannot afford to have companions who won't remain when the conditions are dire. We had all volunteered to be there, and we could all volunteer to leave. Every bit of training we received as SEALs we'd chosen. We didn't get to pick what happened next, but we did choose to be there to take it. We endured as a matter of choice.

Everybody wants to be in charge on a sunny day! Leadership is not bathing in the glory of your Team's effort. It is not reaping the spoils of a great day on the job. Leadership is accepting and enduring the hard and trying times. As a leader, you must relish the tough times. You must take control of adversity and turn it into circumstances you and your Team can live with.

The position of a leader entails the responsibilities associated with being a mentor and role model. You will get calls late at night. You will have to return early from a family function to handle a blossoming problem. You must be a leader for the duration and in every instance, because consistency is paramount to your credibility and the efficient functioning of your team. Your fortitude and stoicism will carry the Team through the tough times. Your example and commitment will be the life ring your people cling to in times of strife.

Moreover, the leadership role is *voluntary*. You may need a job and an income, but your decision to be a leader rather than a follower was strictly your choice. When you accepted the position, whether consciously or not, you recognized the added and daunting responsibilities associated with it.

Leadership is a journey, not a goal! Rely on the basics and a strong foundation. The principles of repetition of Team duties and recording lessons learned will be integral to your success. Find a point in any exercise or Team function to which Team members can return for a fresh start or "systems check." If step three becomes a stumbling point, return to step two. Don't be afraid to repeat work or thought processes if it will help you toward your Team and individual goals.

Leadership is about effecting change for the betterment of your organization. Provide your Team with a vision and attainable goals and guide its members in their pursuit of success. Your Team is your implement with which to make a difference, and it is your duty to make sure your Team members are taken care of properly. Remember, your responsibility as a leader goes beyond the simple meeting of standards. You must challenge and motivate your Team. You must provide the mentorship and professional development to help them achieve a greater level of accomplishment and fulfillment.

If you treat your Team members with respect and remain cognizant of their needs, they will, as a Team, become a satisfied and fulfilled entity. Take the time to find out who is working for you. Though you will periodically have to ask individual members to sacrifice for the Team, always remember that each member is human and has individual needs—career, personal, and otherwise—that must be met for them to be an effective part of your organization.

Take the time and energy to discover strengths and weaknesses in each of your people and to utilize each individual where they will be happy and most effective. Your Teammates will be more dedicated and innovative when they are dealing with familiar and appealing material. You must use your personnel wisely. Do not waste your Team's time and effort on frivolous tasks. Busywork is not ever appropriate. If you assign someone a task, even as extra instruction, make sure it has a useful outcome.

Your Team must know where you are coming from. Leadership is not a game, and people are not mind readers. Make your goals, rules, and expectations clear. Share your vision and explain how you plan to achieve it. In your construction and implementation of that vision, keep your self-image in perspective. Understand that you are in charge, but temper your actions with the realization that though you are the leader, you are still a member of the Team.

Keep a logbook or computer file with all your notes and lessons learned. When you encounter a familiar problem, you can avoid reliving tragedy as you attempt to solve it. I am sure you will think that you'll remember all the lessons, just as I assured myself I could. But you should keep the file handy and leave your memory and brainpower available for more important tasks!

Fortune is to be shared. Success is empty if it is not proliferated. In the SEALs, when someone figures out a new and better way, you share it. When you are promoted and start receiving a bigger paycheck, you take your Teammates out for a treat. You can always find a flyer advertising free beer for Team guys courtesy of a newly paid of promoted SEAL. It is a way to say, "I am successful because of the Team, for if not for the efforts of all, I would not be enjoying these accoutrements!"

The wonderful aspect of leadership is that your style, vision, goal, and situation are yours to mold. Stick to the basics and flavor your style with your life experiences. If you expect hard work from your Team, you must exemplify the sterling work ethic to be emulated. Never be satisfied with your current model. You must continually develop your Teammates and your leadership tactics.

The path of the true Team leader is arduous, but when executed with forethought and vision, it provides bountiful rewards, both material and personal, an experience beyond comprehension. What you get from your Team will be directly related to what you give to it.

People often ask why I became and remain a SEAL. My answer, "It's fun." I believe in one rule: If it sucks, it will make a great story. If it goes smoothly, you are doing something right—but most important, have a great time doing it!

## Concluding Lesson

➢ Be a great leader.

➢ Build a great Team.

➢ Have a great time!